RIDE IT!

The Complete Book of

FLAT TRACK RACING

Gerald Foster

Haynes

Printed and bound in England by the publishers

Published by
The Haynes Publishing Group
Sparkford
Yeovil
Somerset BA22 7JJ
England

Distributed in North America by
Haynes Publications Inc.
861 Lawrence Drive
Newbury Park
California 91320
USA

a FOULIS MOTORCYCLING BOOK — **ISBN 0 85429 232 2**

Editor Jeff Clew
Production/Design Tim Parker with Annette Cutler
Illustration Terry Davey

TO KASS AND SAM

Acknowledgements————————

I am indebted to many people for their input towards this book and I would like to thank them 'up front' for giving so freely of their time, knowledge, and expertise.

To Gene Romero, C.R. (Ax) Axtell, and Mike Libby a special thank you, your help was invaluable.

To Jim Brown, Matt Guzzetta, Don Vesco, Murray Hoffman, Lyle Parker, Bud Ekins, Paul Hunt, Lynn Kastan, Al Fox, Walt Mahony, Steve Levi, Geoff Burgess, Ray Brumbeloe, Ron Wood, Bob Jackson, Russ Sanford, Jim Brucker of Movieworld - Cars of the Stars, David Itterman of the R.J. Reynolds Tobacco Co., Bill Amick of the AMA, and last but not least the AMA for allowing me to reprint some of their material, I thank you.

Gerald Foster
Glendale
California 91201
USA

Contents

Scott Brelsford *(Dan Mahony)*

Preface

Traffic on the freeway travels nose to tail at fifty miles an hour every night during rush hour. Going south from downtown can be a frustrating experience; it is especially bad on a Friday night when everyone appears anxious to get home sooner than usual, to enjoy every minute of the weekend.

Brake lights flash on ahead, necessitating slowing to walking pace.

'Hurry, hurry.'

The traffic crawls for no apparent reason.

'Oh come on you guys, we'll miss the first race.'

Within a mile the freeway has regained momentum; a car motionless and only partly on the shoulder indicates the reason for the hold up.

'I think we can make it in time.'

Floodlights surrounding the oval track can be seen before the offramp is reached. Indicate. Change lanes. Exit. The madness of the freeway is suddenly left behind, yet the surface streets are full of cars and motorcycles, converging on the lights that illuminate the now almost dark sky.

Waiting in line at the ticket booth one notices it is not an attractive place; too much corrugated steel and flaked white paint. But, right now, this is the place to be. Money changes hands. Everyone strolls leisurely towards the entrance until the warm night air is shattered by the staccato of motorcycle engines coming to life. Now there is a rush for seats. Conversations are forgotten. Feet are stomped on. Beer is spilt.

The noise settles down to a steady thunder as the machines are lined up on the starting grid for the first race. Men and boys riding large displacement four-stroke twins, with lots of horse-power and virtually no braking system that could pass any official test.

The starter moves to his platform. Blue smoke hangs in the air above the starting area. Clutches engage. The noise reaches a crescendo, the flag is waved and the bikes explode forward. The crowd roars its approval and the race to the first corner is on.

It is only a heat race, yet the pace is fast and furious. Someone with a three bike length lead on the back straight suddenly finds himself relegated to third place as first one and then another passes on the entry to the corner. As they slide through the corner onto the starting straight the crowd stands as one, craning necks for a better view.

Whoomph! Whoomph! Whoomph! Whoomph! A slight pause. Whoomph! Whoomph! The deep throated exhaust noise of the leading machines bounces off the retaining wall down the straight. The riders are so close that it is almost impossible to separate where noise from one machine ends and another begins.

They circulate until the white flag is brought out, constantly swapping and reswapping positions. But as the bunch enters the last lap there seems to be a definite hunching of shoulders and an aggressiveness which shows in the way the helmeted heads are set. No change coming out of the first corner. On the back straight three riders move up to challenge. Five men enter

Preface

1975 Grand National Champion Gary Scott gets a hole shot over Gene Romero (3) and Rick Hocking (13)
(Bob Jackson)

the last corner in a group. The crowd are cheering on their favorites. It's handlebar to handlebar, as no one intends to give way. Out of the corner come five riders, three line abreast, the other two tucked in close behind. Only the tops of the helmets can be seen, for in an effort to gain maybe half a mile an hour over the other, all are crouched down over the gas tank, cheating the wind.

The rider closest to the wall has perhaps half a wheel at the finish. Only those directly in line could see who finished second and third. Groans are intermingled with the cheers as the crowd regain their seats. This is only the beginning. There will be many more races like this before the night is over.

Bandits at six o'clock, just follow me in. Kenny Roberts leads his 'wing' down the straight at San
(*Bob Jackson*)

A scene like this may take place in your town on a Friday night, or for that matter any night, as flat track racing is a popular sport with both competitors and spectators alike. You may watch the star names of the National circuit or the novices and juniors of your particular area, but with either group everyone is assured of good racing.

Preface

Even the flagman gets in on the act *(Bob Jackson)*

Professional racers are special people. For sometimes they need blind faith and/or stupidity to carry on against insurmountable odds. A culmination of who knows how many hours spent building and tuning a fine piece of machinery to take on the best in the country. The end of many hours spent behind the wheel, driving across the country; of bad hamburgers, muddy coffee and limited budgets. Hopefully the end of a string of bad luck, when nickel and dime parts kept breaking. The racetrack is where it all comes together.

Part of the large crowd that enjoys flat track racing at stadium and fairground tracks around the country
(Bob Jackson)

As motocross has been Europe's gift to the United States, flat track racing is America's unopened gift to the World, for it is a branch of the sport that is unique to North America, commanding both respect and attention at home and abroad. The American Motorcycle Association's National Champion has to be proficient at various forms of racing: road racing, short track, and TT's, but the majority of races on the calender each year are the flat track events, on half-mile and mile length tracks. A factory ride is something to strive for and the National Champion earns the right to carry the Number 1 plate on his bike all year.

Through the pages of this book I hope to increase your knowledge, and hence your interest in the sport, by presenting a look at professional racing, the men and machines. But hold on, I haven't forgotten anyone who wishes to take up the sport for included is information on how to get started, preparation and technique.

This then is flat track racing USA style - a unique experience in sight and sound.

Preface

To the winner go the spoils *(Bob Jackson)*

1 It all began.....

When looking at the United States from the European side of the Atlantic Ocean, I was never able to understand why, after men started racing motorcycles at the turn of the century, did the type of racing practised there (and now for me, here) go off at a totally different tangent to that of Europe. After all, both sides were racing on wooden tracks soon after the turn of the century, the machines were almost identical with large displacement engines popular on both continents, and that Americans were competitive even in the early days of road racing is evidenced by the Indian factory's sweep of the 1911 Isle of Man TT. Further, there was American Jake de Rosier's overall win against the then best rider of England, Charlie Collier, in three head to head races during the same summer, on the 2.75 mile paved and banked Brooklands track near Weybridge, England. How was it then the United States went it's own way in developing a form of racing - flat track, also called dirt track - which no one else practises?

The answer, of course, is locked away in those long forgotten first decades, which some now refer to as the 'Good Old Days', but which in reality were probably terrible because they included a world war and a disastrous depression. Both had an effect on motorcycling and racing.

There really isn't too much written down. Motorcycle racing wasn't as popular a sport in the United States as has been, for instance, baseball, and much of what existed has been destroyed, lost, or is still locked away in scrap books, the pages of which are by now stuck together. Although old tattered and dog-eared sepia photographs record what took place, much of the history of the early years is simply a result of information from the very few people still alive who participated, or which was passed along by word of mouth from those whose father was the friend of a friend who knew ...

There is no magic about how motorcycle racing started, it just had to be. Down through time, the competitive urge has always been there, whether it be man running against man, horse against horse, dog against dog or a crazy combination of any or none of the above. Motorcycles were manufactured, so it was only natural they would be raced. Though they played no part in or had any bearing upon actual racing, endurance runs are worth recalling, for they constitute part of American motorcycle history.

Criss-crossing the country from border to border, or coast to coast, was a good way by which a manufacturer could prove his wares and a rider prove himself. With the continent of North America only just becoming 'civilized', as compared to 'old' Europe, the runs were indeed feats of endurance, as there were virtually no roads outside of the large cities. The land west of the Mississippi was still somewhat of an unknown quantity, with gasoline irregularly available, as was water. Then there was the heat and cold of the deserts, sand or mud which bogged down the wheels, the Rocky Mountains, and, last but not least, occasional unfriendly inhabitants. In addition to all the spares and tools needed, it wasn't unusual for the endurance rider to have about his person, or strapped to his machine, a firearm.

In 1914, a time of eleven and a half days was considered exceptional for the 3000 mile plus trip, but in the years following, days were whittled off the total by virtue of the bikes becoming

It all began.....

more sophisticated and the appearance of better roads, which came with the internal combustion engine revolution. While a sedate three-day drive is now considered the norm for an automobile crossing of the continent, when out in the emptiness of the western states it isn't hard to envisage what the record breaker must have endured for days on end, in his race against the clock to the Atlantic or Pacific Ocean.

As far back as 1906, organized racing under the banner of the Federation of American Motorcyclists was taking place on oval dirt tracks used primarily for horse racing. The tracks were already in existence and as there were no roads to race on (indeed, as we have seen, there were few roads), they made ideal substitutes. There was factory involvement, but motorcycle racing in its infancy didn't attract too much attention from anyone, except a hardcore of enthusiasts. It took a man with a certain amount of vision, flair for the dramatic and an eye for a buck, to get motorcycle racing off and running. That man was Jack Prince, his idea - Motordromes - oval wooden bowls varying from one-quarter to one-half mile around, on which the lap speeds averaged around 90 miles an hour.

The idea wasn't entirely new. Board tracks called 'Velodromes' had been in use for years to hold bicycle and motorcycle races, but Prince took the design a stage further, building much steeper walls, then allowing the paying public to sit in grandstands or stand around the rim, to watch the racing.

Newark Motordrome showing the lack of protection between the riders and spectators

He opened the first Motordrome in 1908 and the result was an instantaneous success. With crowds rolling in to see the racers battling elbow to elbow, the sound of hammers pounding on nails could soon be heard in big cities all across the country. We might now consider that the early advertisements reduced motorcycle racing to a freak or carnival show atmosphere, for the words 'daredevils' and 'spectacle' were used frequently and many of the tracks were intentionally built in, or adjacent to, amusement parks. Yet, irrespective of what it took to get the people in, they enjoyed the league team racing once inside and continuously came back for more.

The wooden tracks were marvels of engineering and even today would still be so considered. Consisting of a huge framework over which were laid literally thousands of 2 in by 4 in boards, each track must have cost its owner a fortune. Some were banked as much as forty or fifty degrees, and while the surface had to be left rough for traction, the corners were carefully blended into the straights, to provide a smooth surface.

There were dirt track events during the popular years of the board tracks, even some big ones, but compared to the popularity of the boards, this branch of the sport was on the back burner. It was, however, destined to be moved up to the front burner in later years, for as factories strived for victories on the oval wooden tracks, serious accidents became the order of the day. The spindly framed, narrow tired 1000cc V-twins became too powerful for the small tracks and the ever increasing speeds imposed problems for which technology had no immediate answer. Tires couldn't stand the punishment, neither could the bicycle type frames. Boards became slippery by virtue of oil being laid down from the total loss lubrication systems and

A 1915 overhead cam 61cu. in. V-twin Cyclone, one of only about thirty ever built. Reputedly, the factory machines were so fast that on occasions all other teams packed up and went home, rather than race against them *(Author)*

Kansas City Speedway, one of the longer, safer board tracks, which were built in the 1920s *(The AMA)*

More action on one of the longer super speedway type board tracks *(The AMA)*

It all began.....

falling on the rough planks was something else again. With no protective helmets, head injuries were a serious problem, as were the splinters which gouged into the flesh of any rider who had the misfortune to fall and slide along the boards. The carnage made headlines to the extent local authorities were pressured into closing down many of the tracks.

The changeover didn't occur overnight; it was a gradual process which took years. After the first world war there were still races on wooden tracks, this time automobile tracks which were wider, safer and longer (up to 2 miles) than the old Motordromes, but by the early thirties the board tracks had all closed up, due in part to the depression and heavy maintenance costs. The first chapter of American motorcycle racing was coming to an end. If, up until then, there had been some exchange of competition with the riders of Europe, it was to be lost when the emphasis was placed solely on dirt track racing.

Racing in Europe from its inception had always meant 'road racing'. When roads were no longer permitted to be closed off for races, the paved courses were simply 'transplanted' onto private property, to become closed race tracks in their own right. While the boards were popular in America, the machines and style of racing had run a parallel course to that of Europe. With only dirt track racing, a point had been reached where the similarity ceased; development of style and machines went off in opposed directions. Whereas the quickest way around a dirt oval required a foot down sliding technique, the road racer kept his feet up. The feet up brigade found their type of racing better suited to dropped handlebars, while the sliders turned to a wider more upswept type to wrestle the V-twins around the ovals. Road race courses required brakes; no brakes were required in dirt tracking. And, of course, European engines began shrinking in size compared to those of their American brothers.

If any one reason can be given as to why American racing didn't follow the pattern already set in Europe, perhaps it is only that there were no winding roads to be shut off for racing and the majority were still dirt anyway. The thinking concerning roads which still prevails today is that the shortest and quickest way from point A to point B is a straight line, irrespective of what has to be gone over, dug out or tunneled through to do it. Excellent for a communications network, the roads nevertheless were unsuitable for racing. If a promoter of the caliber of Jack Prince had built road race courses, promoting them as he had done the board tracks, the racing might have followed different lines. However, the emphasis shifted to racing Americans already knew - dirt track - yet it almost foundered before really getting started. In a squeeze because of the economic situation, the factories withdrew much of the support on which professional racing depended, and by the late 1920's motorcycle racing was experiencing difficulties.

This 1922 Harley-Davidson saw action on board and dirt tracks *(Author)*

18

This 1923 45cu. in. Indian was good for 126mph in the hands of Freddie Ludlow *(Bob Jackson)*

In order to save the sport, a different set of rules which eliminated the specialized machinery and professionalism were introduced by the American Motorcycle Association, the newly formed governing body. The class 'A' and 'B' factory specials of the Federation of American Motorcyclists were banned, and only authentic production machines were allowed. Designated class 'C', the basic concept, with notable changes, is still in force today. While any full-fledged professional might find it hard to make a living, the racing suited the amateur, as with very little outlay he could race his street bike on weekends. So began a type of racing with which Europeans have always had trouble identifying. The idea has been to provide close, competitive racing on near identical machines, at a cost which everyone could afford, with the rider making the difference. Soon after class 'C' racing was introduced, the governing bodies of American and European racing fell out with each other and went their separate ways. The Europeans did not consider production bike racing served the best interest of the sport. Maybe it was shades of the revolution still lingering for it seems some on the European side never really got over the fact that a country could secede of its own free will. I am now sure some of this animosity trickled down over the years (whether intentionally or not) through the motorcycle press and was in part the reason for holding dirt track racing in such low regard. Even up until the late sixties, when calmer heads prevailed, any European rider participating in any sanctioned AMA event (if he could or wanted to) risked his license being revoked.

When looked at from the American side, there was simply no alternative. They were in a do or die situation to save the sport and the industry; class 'C' racing hopefully would do it. What was the value in keeping ties with any organization which wanted to regulate them, when there was no similarity in the machines or the racing?

In the early days of flat track racing, racers and bikes adapted to the equine way of racing. Up until, and even when automobiles became mass produced, America was horse country, but horse country in a way Europe was not. Instead of being a refined animal owned by moneyed people, the American horse was a work animal, a mode of transportation which tolerated the elements, and a race horse which could run over almost any surface. State or county fairgrounds, which always included a horse track, were simply meeting places for racing the animals.

It all began.....

Early dirt track racing at Portland, Oregon, shows just how much of a problem dust was to the early racers

Although holes, ripples and ridges didn't bother sure footed horses, they and the dust posed problems for the motorcycle racers. The almost unsprung machines, holding V-twin engines, bucked like broncos around the corners, enveloping everyone, including the spectators, in dust, and the dust posed even greater problems if a rider caught an 'edge' and fell.

The machines and the tracks improved over the years, but there is little doubt that American motorcycle development lagged behind that of Europe until the sport again became professionalized in the early fifties. The appearance of foreign-made machines, technically superior, helped speed up the process, and with more prize money available there was a new awakening.

Although the AMA Grand National series proper started only in 1954, from 1946 onwards, when racing resumed after World War II, the country had a National Motorcycle Champion every year. An indication of how much simpler things were back then, the title and the right to carry the Number 1 plate hinged on the outcome of one particular race - the Springfield, Illinois, 50 lapper on a mile track.

While flat track racing is still the premier type of racing in the United States, the object of the Grand National Championship series has been since its inception to crown America's most

Ed Kretz on an Indian at the 100 mile National at Langhorne, Pennsylvania, during the 1940s *(The AMA)*

versatile motorcycle racer. There are other types of racing which make up the series and these are covered briefly in the following chapter.

Before investigating the current state of the sport, some background information on American motorcycle manufacturers is in order. The industry, like that of England, once numbered many individual companies, the majority of which have faded into obscurity. Of the giants who were racing in the early days, only one - Harley-Davidson - is still around today.

In America motorcycles never really enjoyed the affection automobiles enjoyed, primarily because the cheap mass produced four wheelers became available at the time when motorcycles were just becoming established. The public fell in love with the automobile, to the detriment of the motorcycle. Unfortunately, the motorcycle was not the less expensive stepping stone to automobile ownership as it was, for instance, in England. Consequently, many of their manufacturers fell on hard times, ultimately to close their doors forever.

Three names have always stood out in American motorcycle racing: Indian, Harley-Davidson, and Excelsior. We tend to look in awe at the Japanese racing machines of the sixties which had four valves per cylinder, yet it is interesting to note that very early 61 cu.in. Indian V-twin Motordrome racers also used the same layout. The old adage of there being nothing new under the sun is certainly true of motorcycle design.

Though Indian and Excelsior profited from racing, their ultimate undoing was either the depression or machines which were technically unsound and no one wanted anyway. Excelsior succumbed in 1931, the Indian company some twenty years later. Harley-Davidson's seemingly charmed life has been due in part to being a conservative company through the good as well as the bad times, offering the buying public basically what it wanted - big, loping, go-all-day V-twins.

Through the WR, the first real production race bike, the KR and the present XR models, Harley-Davidson has been quietly improving the V-twin. At times development may seemingly have stagnated and needed to be given a push onwards by such intruders as the Manx Norton and the BSA Gold Star. Nevertheless, the current XR750 models have reached the enviable

Chet Dykgraaff (5) became the first National Champion when racing continued in 1946 after World War 2. *(The AMA)*. From 1946 through 1953 the National Championship was awarded to the winner of one race — a 50 lapper on the mile track at Springfield, Illinois

It all began.....

Above Joe Leonard (98) became the AMA's first Grand National Champion in 1954 when he won eight races of the inaugeral championship. No longer would a single race decide the championship; only the most versatile racers would have the chance to carry the covetted No. 1 plate *(Dan Mahony)*

Below Bart Markel known affectionately as 'Bad Bart' is considered by many the greatest dirt tracker of them all. He captured National titles in 1962, 1965 and 1966 racking up a total of 28 National wins *(Dan Mahony)*

Above left Ken Roberts — Grand National Champion in 1973 and 1974 *(Bob Jackson)*

Above right Gary Scott — Grand National Champion 1975 *(Bob Jackson)*

Below For what he lacks in horsepower Roberts makes up in determination *(Bob Jackson)*

It all began.....

Above Unable to agree on terms with Harley-Davidson for the 1976 season, Scott rode as a privateer on a variety of machines. The unmarked machine is a Harley-Davidson *(Bob Jackson)*

Top left (inset) Jay Springsteen — the 1976 Grand National Champion — is at nineteen one of the youngest riders to capture the title *(Bob Jackson)*

Right Rookie of the year in 1975, as a privateer, Springsteen's ability to get back on the gas early in the corners quickly made him a force to be reckoned with *(Bob Jackson)*

It all began.....

position of being the most powerful and reliable twin cylinder machines used in dirt track competition.

No look at American motorcycle racing would be complete without mention of some of the past and present all time greats, whose names have been etched into the record book.

Joe Petrali, a factory rider for Excelsior and Harley-Davidson in the twenties and thirties, made his mark, for he was good at everything. There were others, such as Ralph Hepburn and Jim Davis, plus many more who are now forgotten. After World War II, Chet Dykgraff became the first National Champion, by virtue of his win at Springfield on a Norton. Then Jimmy Chann took over for three years, on a Harley-Davidson.

1954, the first year of National Championship Series proper, saw Joe Leonard walk off with the title - as he did in 1956 and 1957 before turning his attention to a successful motor racing career.

Many argue Carroll Resweber never realized his full potential, but he did win four consecutive titles in 1958, 1959, 1960 and 1961. Late in the '62 season, on his way to a fifth title, a serious racing accident forced his early retirement.

Bart Markel, known affectionately as 'Bad Bart', Dick Mann, Roger Reiman, Gary Nixon, Mert Lawwill and Gene Romero shared the years 1962 through 1971. Markel, a great flat tracker who captured titles in 1962, 1965 and 1966, considers himself only semi-retired, for he will don a set of leathers if the notion takes him. Dick Mann, an all-around specialist and Champion in 1963 and 1971, is attributed with making the swing arm work on flat tracks whereas no one else could. Gary Nixon, a favorite with the spectators, won back to back titles in 1967 and 1968, but serious injuries have also marred his career. 1969 Champion Mert Lawwill, now 36, is still campaigning the title chase, as is Gene Romero, the 1970 Champion. 1972 was Mark Brelsford's year; however, a crash at the following year's Daytona road race and a leg fracture with near fatal complications the following year ended another brilliant career.

Boyish looking Kenny Roberts was the star of the 1973 and 1974 seasons, with three-time runner up Gary Scott taking the title in 1975. As the 1975 title chase was a cliff hanger throughout the later part of the season, Chapter 7 has been devoted to the racing, the machinery and the eventual outcome.

1976 was the year in which one of the youngest ever riders took home the Number 1 plate. Jay Springsteen, a nineteen year old factory Harley-Davidson rider from Michigan, achieved his success by winning seven National events on the dirt in only his second year on the National Circuit.

That only thirteen riders have held the prestigious Number One plate since 1954 is verification of how hard it is to master the different types of dirt tracks (and road tracks, too). However, of those who never made it, Cal Rayborn deserves mentioning. A spectacular rider from San Diego, California, Rayborn was considered to be one of the greats, not only by the spectators but the most critical of peers - other professionals. He was a spectacular miler and a superb road racer, but although he placed third in the standings twice, he was never to achieve the title as an unfortunate accident during a race in Australia cut short his life.

As American motorcycle racing, like its counterparts in other countries, has been thru rough times to match the good times, the inevitable question has to be 'How healthy is flat track racing?' The answer: 'Quite healthy.' There are at present a limited number of machines and engines available, with which to race, yet more people are watching than ever before. With some newer manufacturers entering the smaller displacement class, the future looks bright.

Some of the 'old timers' who rode in the fifties deplore how the racing has changed in that the original intent of class 'C' racing has been circumvented with the AMA's approval. But even if the sport is more expensive (what isn't?) and specialized (what isn't?), it certainly isn't dull. And, if years ago the average rider stood a chance of taking home some money, he still does today, for even if the rules have become more liberal, they are still the same for everyone. Some riders are limited by the amount of money they can spend; yet, having a factory Harley-Davidson guarantees a rider nothing. In fact, many privately owned H.D.'s are as fast, maybe even a shade faster, than the factory bikes.

There are many sports and even other types of motorcycle racing where it is possible to predict the outcome before the race has been run. This is not so with flat tracking, which, in part, may be why it is so popular. At every National race, there are some ten or twelve riders lined up at the start who can win, and the outcome is impossible to predict until the checkered flag is waved. So hot is the competition and urge to win there has been almost fifty lead changes in a twenty five mile race.

With the competition so fierce, drafting or slipstreaming plays a major part on the mile tracks and is one of the reasons so many lead changes are possible. Even before a corner is completely exited, the riders will have the left foot back on the peg, be crouched down over the tank and tucked in as close as possible behind the machine ahead, in order to catch a tow in the still air. The faster bikes will move ahead down the straights, but done correctly, drafting

Above In the 1950s and 60s the Mecca for all aspiring dirt trackers *(Bob Jackson)*

Below The current state of the art. In many instances a blanket would cover the first six, eight, and sometimes ten riders *(Bob Jackson)*

It all began.....

enables those down on power to keep up. There is also a lot of overtaking in the corners and anyone who errs slightly off the racing line will testify to the fact that someone is always ready and waiting to slip by, only inches away.

Now drafting and swapping positions going into and around corners may not seem out of the ordinary to followers of road racing, but there is a difference. The surface is dirt, speeds down the straights exceed 130mph, brakes as a rule aren't used to scrub off the excess speed, and everyone is sliding handlebar to handlebar, which leaves no room for mistakes. In many instances, a blanket can cover the first six, eight, sometimes ten riders and this is how complete races are run at 95mph lap speeds. In a majority of races, first place is decided only on the run from the last corner to the flag. Yes, mile racing is a fantastic sight.

Whenever the subject of half-mile racing crops up, the name of one track - Ascot Park in Gardena - will eventually enter the conversation. Ascot is a synonymous with half-mile racing. During the fifties and sixties many riders from all over the country emigrated with bikes and belongings (which usually amounted to less than the raceware inventory) to the half-mile mecca.

There was racing for everyone: the novices or first year professionals, juniors who had progressed to the larger machines used by the experts, and, of course, the expert professionals, many of whom followed the National circuit. Because the National race schedule was so much shorter, it wasn't unusual to see a sizeable majority of named professional riders at Ascot each week during the season. They would simply head post haste from wherever the previous Sunday's racing had been, to run Ascot on a Friday night. The crowd was always large, the prize money good and more often than not, with so many entered, the racing went on well into the night. Today, the track does not enjoy the prominence it once did for with the number of National races at virtually one a week, there isn't time for cross country trips to fit in Friday nights at Ascot.

As there are more half-mile tracks available for use around the country, this type of racing constitutes a good portion of the National schedule. If racing on mile tracks is the 'caviar' of flat tracking, then half-mile racing is the 'icing on the cake'. The corners are tighter and there is no emphasis on drafting, yet the lap speeds are still up around 70mph, which translates in straightaway speeds in excess of 90mph.

In his van, the professional racer is a modern day gypsy, who will wander around the country several times between January and when the season finishes in October. Many hanker after the glamorous life, for it is a job which requires no nine to five routine. But while there are less limitations and restrictions to a racing career, the life, like any other, is governed by pressures and clocks. Unlike professionals in other countries, the American rider on the National circuit cannot rely on start or appearance money for the bulk of his earnings. Money is paid out for appearances in minor meets, and factory riders are on retainers, but the 'pressures' on the majority for staying self-employed are in the main repeatedly good performances, showing up as a healthy payout at the end of a day's racing. The 'clocks', unlike those in our lives, measure time in tenths of seconds, which can be the difference in qualifying or not qualifying for the program, or in many instances, the interval by which a race is won.

Though some might consider it a sad mirror of the times we live in, the subject of earnings will always crop up. The current National Champion now earns in excess of $100,000 (£60,000) gross, but certainly no more than $200,000 (£120,000). Many get by on far, far less. Prize money has increased over the years and contingency awards from manufacturers and companies who support the sport has done much in sweetening the pot. Perhaps the biggest coup has been sponsorship of the complete National series to the tune of $100,000 (£60,000) by the R.J. Reynolds Tobacco Company, which explains why the Grand National Series is also known as the 'Camel Pro Series'.

In preparing this brief look at the sport, I have been painfully aware of the many people who played a part over the years yet have not been mentioned. However, I am sure no one past or present will begrudge the space I am about to give to a pretty, 20 year old girl from Salem, Oregon.

Diane Cox is a fresh breeze blowing through the hallowed halls of what have been described

It all began.....

Left The new racers? 19 year old Diane Cox is the first — and to date — the only licensed female expert professional in AMA racing *(Bob Jackson)*

Below Diane Cox (66) on a borrowed machine, much faster than her own, during a 1976 Trophy race at San Jose, California *(Bob Jackson)*

vaguely in the past as 'men only' sports. She is the first, and to date, the only AMA expert licensed female motorcycle racer in the United States. Appearing at selected Nationals, she has often qualified in the top third of the entry, and has on a number of occasions only barely missed making the National final.

While Diane may strike fear into some of her male competitors, the spectators love her.

To my mind her most stirring performance occured at the last mile race of the 1976 season at San Jose, California, when she again just missed getting into the National Final through semi-final competition. By virtue of her semi-final finish, she put herself on the first row for the Trophy Race. On a very rapid Harley-Davidson borrowed from Gary Scott, she worked her way up to second place within striking distance of the first slot. In an effort to win, she actually caught the leader on the last corner, but had gone in too fast and fell.

While all this was taking place, the large crowd which filled the grandstand was on its feet cheering wildly for the girl from Oregon. Virtually every head remained rivetted on the far

It all began.....

away corner as medical personnel checked to make sure she was okay. Then a huge cheer went up when she was seen to stand and commence the long walk back to the pits. I mention this as during these few minutes the winner - and to this day, to my shame I do not know his name - was being presented with his trophy in front of the grandstand. No one took the slightest notice.

Diane Cox has proved women are viable competitors and no doubt others will eventually follow her lead.

Move over guys!

GRAND NATIONAL CHAMPION

1946	Chet Dykgraff	NOR	
1947	Jimmy Chann	H-D	Title and No.1 Plate won at
1948	Jimmy Chann	H-D	Springfield, Illinois
1949	Jimmy Chann	H-D	
1950	Larry Headrick	H-D	
1951	Bobby Hill	IND	
1952	Bobby Hill	IND	
1953	Bill Tuman	IND	
1954	Joe Leonard	H-D	76 points
1955	Brad Andres	H-D	80
1956	Joe Leonard	H-D	32
1957	Joe Leonard	H-D	41
1958	Carroll Resweber	H-D	36
1959	Carroll Resweber	H-D	52
1960	Carroll Resweber	H-D	49
1961	Carroll Resweber	H-D	62
1962	Bart Markel	H-D	58
1963	Dick Mann	BSA-MAT	114
1964	Roger Reiman	H-D	503
1965	Bart Markel	H-D	620
1966	Bart Markel	H-D	434
1967	Gary Nixon	TRI	508
1968	Gary Nixon	TRI	622
1969	Mert Lawwill	H-D	672
1970	Gene Romero	TRI	667
1971	Dick Mann	BSA	1054
1972	Mark Brelsford	H-D	1483
1973	Ken Roberts	YAM	2014
1974	Ken Roberts	YAM	2286
1975	Gary Scott	H-D	1358
1976	Jay Springsteen	H-D	301

Grand National Champion of the American Motorcycle Association is a term which originated in 1954 with the establishment of the AMA Grand National Champion Series, a circuit including competition on paved road courses and dirt tracks of all varieties. Previously (1946 to 1953) the winner of the traditional race at Springfield, Illinois, was named National Champion.

2 Is that all there is to a National Championship?

TO BE A PROFESSIONAL MOTORCYCLE RACER IN SEARCH OF POINTS FOR THE COVETTED US NUMBER 1 PLATE IS TO KNOW THE SUSPENSION CRUSHING BANKING AT THE DAYTONA ROAD RACE, THE JUMP ON THE ASCOT TT COURSE, THE ONE HUNDRED MILE AN HOUR CORNERS ON THE INDIANAPOLIS MILE, AND THE SHORT TRACK COURSE IN THE CAVERNOUS HOUSTON ASTRODOME. THE UNITED STATES IS THE ONLY COUNTRY THAT EXPECTS ITS GRAND NATIONAL CHAMPION CONTEN—DERS TO BE PROFICIENT AT MORE THAN JUST ONE FORM OF MOTOR—CYCLE RACING.

Considering how specialized motorcycle racing has become around the world (and in the US) in that there are National and World Championships for different types of motorcycle competition, it may be considered madness to expect a man to be proficient at the various forms of the sport which make up the Grand National series. But this is how it is, and surprisingly there are quite a few riders who are as comfortable with such techniques as knee dragging in road racing and the foot sliding of flat tracking.

Although flat track, short track, and TT events bear a resemblance to each other in that they are all classed as dirt track events, road racing is in a league of its own. A separate National Road Race Championship series proposed by many could possibly materialize in 1978 or 1979 (maybe even later) to the delight of road race enthusiasts and riders, but to the disgust of some Grand National contenders who like and enjoy the challenges of the varied types of racing which make the American Championship scene so unique.

Over the past few years the number of road races on the National circuit has been declining, reaching a low of four in 1976. Two more have been added for 1977 and not a moment too soon, for with rider participation and interest growing, new governing bodies formed solely to promote, and run road races, have been rapidly gaining ground in filling the void.

With so little road racing interspersed among the dirt track events, the proposal to run a separate National Championship seems a logical one, for then the number of races could be increased, opening up the field to many riders who have neither the money nor the inclination for flat tracking. Currently this is what happens in reverse, for many flat trackers do not like the pavement, cannot find a sponsor, or just plain cannot afford the specialized machinery required. Luckily, missing the few road races of late has proved no great disadvantage, as can be seen from the fact that 1976 National Champion Jay Springsteen did not compete in any of the road races. With two more races added however, it is doubtful whether this type of situation can occur in 1977.

Of course many riders like the status quo, and another side of the discussion involving dropping the road racing might be put forth by Kenny Roberts, whose argument could be along the lines of needing road race points to supplement his inadequacies as a dirt track specialist. In this instance nothing could be further from the truth, because Kenny's prowess

Is that all there is to a National Championship?

13 may be unlucky for some, but not Rick Hocking, whose Harley has more than enough power to wheelie at over 100mph *(Bob Jackson)*

Is that all there is to a National Championship?

as a road racer is on a par with his dirt track abilities. Indeed this young man is probably the greatest all-around motorcycle racer the United States has ever seen, and one of the best road racers in the world. Such credentials lay claim to the AMA's original idea of a National Champion being competent at many branches of the sport, and many will mourn the passing of an era when a separate road race championship begins, as no longer will the Champion have to be the complete all arounder he once was.

Problems and politics aside, there is little doubt the quality of all types of professional racing in this country is high. For years we Europeans believed we had it all sewn up, with all of the major championships being decided in Europe. We tended to dismiss flat track racing as some

Below John Gennai *(Dan Mahony)*

Is that all there is to a National Championship?

juvenile form of speedway racing. I can only surmise a lack of communication clouded our vision. Times have changed though with foreign riders competing in the US and vice-versa, but flat track racing still remains exclusively an American preserve with only American participation. Possibly the main reason for the sport never having been 'exported' is that very few long stadium or fairground tracks exist anywhere except in this country Also, all other popular forms of racing in the various countries are now so deeply entrenched that it would take a multi-million dollar Madison Avenue advertising effort in order for it to catch on. And yet interest from abroad is there, for many enthusiasts visiting the US express a wish to see a flat track and go home with only the highest regard for riders who wrestle the big machines at incredible speeds around the dirt tracks.

Although the glamor may be in the mile and half mile flat track races, TTs, short tracks, and road races constitute one half of all the races on the National circuit. They are as widely dispersed around the country as it is possible to get and the competition is as keen as for the mile and half mile races. Let us now examine these other forms of racing, which are also an important part of the AMA Grand National title chase.

ROAD RACING

Although road racing does not enjoy the prominence in the United States it does in other countries, the National meetings nevertheless draw many thousands of spectators. Courses and race lengths vary but all share combinations of right and left-hand turns and high speed straightaways. Daytona, in Florida, is a prime example of a speed course, with riders reaching 180mph on the straights and not much less in the steep 30 degree banked corners which form part of the course. The centrifugal force on the banking is so great that front and rear suspensions are completely compressed, giving the riders an extremely rough, teeth chattering, vision impairing ride. Because of the high speeds, tire wear became a critical problem at Daytona in 1976 and Kenny Roberts was lucky to escape injury when, with the race almost in his pocket, the rear slick went flat after the rubber and supportive backing had worn completely away. Johnny Cecotto went on to finish first, with his slick in a similar, yet still inflated, condition.

By contrast, Laguna Seca on the Monterey Peninsular in Northern California, is a demanding riders' course where sheer power is not a consideration and tire wear not as an acute a problem. Unlike the majority of road race courses, Laguna Seca has uphills and downhills, which make it more interesting for both riders and spectators alike.

The 750cc formula is common to road race as it is to flat track machines, but four cylinders are allowed in road racing as opposed to only two in flat track. Designed as an over

Grand National road racing *(Bob Jackson)*

Is that all there is to a National Championship?

the counter production racer, and approved by the AMA, the four cylinder TZ750 Yamahas, have, since their introduction, dominated American road racing; in doing so they have forced other manufacturers back to the drawing boards from whence they have not yet returned. Many have argued that racing has suffered as a result, but it is still competitive and the TZs have given the privateer a new lease on life.

As all dirt track racers progress by accumulating points through novice to junior to expert status, so must licensed road racers. However, there are only two grades, novice and expert, and novices are limited to 250cc machinery.

Although the techniques are vastly different many riders are as competent at road racing as they are at dirt tracking *(Bob Jackson)*

Currently the winningest machine in road racing — the Yamaha TZ750 four cylinder two-stroke *(Author)*

Is that all there is to a National Championship?

Steve Baker

   Currently the man of the moment in American road racing, Steve Baker is a quiet bespectacled 23 year old from Bellingham, Washington, who has been spending much of his time road racing in Europe, where he achieved more than considerable success in 1976. He won the Race of the Year at Mallory Park in England, beating 500cc World Champion Barry Sheene, and all time great Giacomo Agostini of Italy. He also won the richest road race in the world, the Italian Imola 200, and the Venezuelan Grand Prix, as well as finding time to win the AMA Grand National races at Loudon, New Hampshire, and Laguna Seca. Like many other AMA Grand National racers, Baker is competent at other forms of racing and when not road racing can turn in pretty good performances on the dirt tracks.

Left Steve Baker *(Author)*

Below The basic differences between this TT machine and a flat tracker are: The more conventionally placed footpegs, the addition of a front brake, an exhaust system which allows the rider to move unobstructed around the machine, and different handlebars *(Author)*

Is that all there is to a National Championship?

TOURIST TROPHY

Tourist Trophy or 'TT', as it is commonly known, is a European term borrowed to describe racing which is a mixture of flat track and motocross.

TT courses are generally about three quarters of a mile in length, have both left and right-hand turns and a jump over which the riders fly thru the air. Usually located at an existing oval track, the course meanders around the infield, with an excursion onto the oval.

Above TT racing under the lights *(Dan Mahony)*

Below Locking back towards the jump on the TT course at Ascot Park *(Dan Mahony)*

Is that all there is to a National Championship?

The 750cc two cylinder limit, plus the rules of flat track, also apply to TT racing, and even the machines are similar. The only exceptions are: front and rear brakes which must be fitted to cater for the different turns and straights, more conventionally placed footpegs on which the rider can stand when negotiating a jump, a tucked in or under exhaust system which allows the rider to clamber around both sides of the machine on left and right-hand corners, and a different style of handlebars.

Chuck Joyner

TT specialists are almost impossible to beat on their homeground and 26 year old Chuck Joyner of Oregon City, Oregon, proved this dramatically by winning the 1976 Castle Rock, Washington, TT for the third time in four years. As short track racing is popular in Texas, so is TT racing in the Pacific Northwest, and evidence of this are three other men: Randy Skiver, Sonny Burres, and Billy Oliver, from Oregon and Washington, who overshadowed the top AMA pros by finishing third, fourth and sixth respectively.

With the majority of the better racers being short and extremely well built around the chest and shoulders, Joyner is the exception at 6 ft 2 in and a spindly 165 lb. He pays his own way, having no sponsor, and although TT's are his speciality, he gives good account of himself on the flat tracks.

Chuck Joyner *(Author)*

SHORT TRACK

Little brother of the mile and half miles, short track racing requires a somewhat different style and smaller capacity machinery, as the oval dirt tracks average only one quarter mile in length. Apart from displacement, which is limited to 250cc single cylinder engines, the machines otherwise resemble the larger bikes. Competition is also as fierce, with riders bumping and banging each other as they jockey for positions on the highly manoeuverable machines.

An advantage to short track racing is that a large indoor facility can accommodate a track and thus the weather outside cannot postpone the racing. The Houston Astrodome is so large that it easily accommodates a National short track event, even a TT, and both these events are held in January, when much of the country is shivering.

Is that all there is to a National Championship?

Above Short track racing in the Houston Astrodome *(Dan Mahony)*

Below The tight quarter mile tracks make for extremely close and competitive racing *(Dan Mahony)*

Is that all there is to a National Championship?

Mike Kidd

Growing up first in midget race cars and then on the short tracks which abound in his native Texas, 5 ft 6 in tall, 130 lb. Mike Kidd turned professional at 17, making expert in two years. His expertise on the short tracks makes him a favorite for a good placing whenever one of the events comes up in AMA Grand National racing, but he was sidelined for much of two seasons when a leg badly broken in 1974 was broken again in 1975. Proving that his ability extends to other areas was one victory and a second place at the back to back Indianapolis miles, on Saturday and Sunday August 28 and 29, 1976.

Mike Kidd *(Author)*

3 It's all down in black and white

EVER WONDERED HOW MUCH PRIZE MONEY IS PAID OUT AT A NATIONAL? DID YOU KNOW ONE RIDER CAN CLAIM THE MACHINE OF ANOTHER? DELVING BELOW THE SURFACE OF AMA PROFESSIONAL RACING IS NOT ALWAYS POSSIBLE FOR THE SPECTATOR WHO SITS ON THE OTHER SIDE OF THE FENCE, OR THE ENTHUSIAST WHO CAN ONLY READ RACE REPORTS IN THE MOTORCYCLE PRESS. WITH THESE FOLKS IN MIND, SOME OF THE MORE INTERESTING AND SALIENT RULES ARE COVERED IN THIS CHAPTER.

LICENSING

In AMA professional racing everyone starts at the bottom as a novice, working upwards thru junior to expert status via a grading system. This grading system is advantageous in that a rider never competes at a higher level than that at which he is competent, essential to the safety of himself and others considering the speeds attained. Advancement out of the novice into the junior class requires an accumulation of 40 points, which are awarded to the first four finishers in heat races, semi finals, and finals. Junior to expert requires another 80 points and it is possible to make expert in two years by riding often and placing consistently.

A license is an annual chore for all groups of riders and an application has to be accompanied by a physicians report. At $55 (£35) a license, including membership of the AMA, isn't cheap, and with the addition of a doctor's examination the final bill is probably up around $100 (£60).

When a license, a plastic type credit card, is issued a medical card accompanies it. The card carries vital information such as blood type, any allergic reactions to medicine etc, and is carried when racing within a pocket of the rider's leathers. Motorcycle racing is dangerous and $100 may seem like an inordinate amount of money, but in the event of an injury that plastic card can be an invaluable aid to the immediate and correct treatment.

Being under twenty one years of age has always had its drawbacks and applying for an AMA professional license is no exception. The rider must be at least sixteen years old and submit a notarized signed release from his parents with the application. The AMA is touchy about law suits which could be initiated by the angry parents of an injured minor who has not received their permission to race.

ENGINE CAPACITY

Most enthusiasts are familiar with the 750cc formula used by experts (and juniors) on half mile, mile and TT courses, but many may not be too conversant with the recent equipment rule changes affecting all three groups in short track racing, and novices in half mile and TT racing, (novices progress to mile tracks after becoming juniors).

Prior to January 1, 1977, all who rode in these events were limited to engines of 250cc

It's all down in black and white

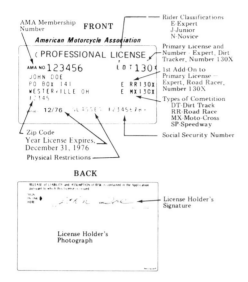

AMA Membership Number

FRONT

Rider Classifications
E-Expert
J-Junior
N-Novice

American Motorcycle Association

PROFESSIONAL LICENSE

AMA NO 123456

JOHN DOE
PO BOX 141
WESTERVILLE OH
43345

12/76

Primary License and Number - Expert, Dirt Tracker, Number 130X

1st Add-On to Primary License — Expert, Road Racer, Number 130X

Types of Cometition
DT-Dirt Track
RR-Road Race
MX-Moto-Cross
SP-Speedway

Zip Code
Year License Expires, December 31, 1976
Physical Restrictions

Social Security Number

BACK

License Holder's Signature

License Holder's Photograph

Above left A line drawing of the plastic credit card type license issued to professional racers *(The AMA)*

Above right The medical card with pertinent information regarding blood group, etc. is kept within a pocket of the leathers *(Author)*

Below Gary Horton at Louisville, Kentucky *(Dan Mahony)*

It's all down in black and white

capacity if a multi-cylinder two-stroke was used, or 360cc for all other types of engines. As of January 1, 1977, a new formula was adopted which has now limited everyone to a single cylinder engine, either two-stroke or four-stroke with a maximum displacement of 250cc.

The reason for changes - to promote safer racing, in one case; the bikes had become too fast for the tracks, and in the other, the bikes were too fast for the riders.

In short track racing the high horsepower 360cc singles proved a little too much for the small tracks, especially since handlebar banging is part of the game. And on half miles the novice lap speeds were becoming faster and faster to the point where the times were not that much slower than those the experts were turning.

The ruling has been a controversial one in that it has incurred additional expense for a vast majority of riders. But while the twins are unusable many of the competitive 360cc singles have been converted to 250cc at a lesser cost than buying a new engine, which is at least some consolation to the many who by necessity race on a budget. Although the best men will still win, many more novices should find the new rule provides them with more opportunities of 'mixing it', something not possible against the 'exotic' twins used under the old ruling.

RACE MEETS

To the first time spectator, a flat track meet might appear unfathomable, with qualifying time trials, sometimes qualifying heats, heats, semi-finals and trophy dash, but in reality it is all very simple.

In an effort to give the novice racers as much racing experience as possible, the rules state they must qualify for the program by racing in heats. As there is always an abundance of novices, a series of qualifying heats, and occasionally semi-finals, are run to whittle down the entry before the actual heat racing begins.

Juniors and experts qualify for the program by running in time trials, and both groups must attempt a run within the time allowed. After one warm up lap, the clocks start timing the second lap. Prior to taking the checkered flag on completion of the second lap, each rider without knowing his time must decide to either accept the lap or wave it off. If he thinks the time could be bettered, giving him a better shot at making the program, a second and last try is allowed later. The number of riders required for the heats are then taken from the fastest qualifier on downwards, until all the berths have been filled.

Because a number of factors governs how many races are to be run, it is impossible to detail any particular program. However, the method of elimination is well standardized and should explain what goes on more easily than using actual numbers.

A number of heats are run and a predetermined number of riders from the winner on down qualify directly for the final. In many but not all meets, one, or two (maybe more according to the number of heats) semi-finals are run, which are a last ditch effort for the next highest placed riders to make the final. As most tracks can only accommodate a maximum of twelve to sixteen riders the number qualifying from either the heats or semis is of necessity small.

In some respects the AMA has misnamed semi-final races, for they are simply 'competition that precedes the final event' and not the more usual 'one of two competitions whereby thru a process of elimination competitors qualify for the final'.

The Trophy Dash, a race run in addition to the regular program, is open to the first four experts with the fastest qualifying times. It sometimes happens that the fastest qualifier does not make a final, so for him the Trophy Dash is a consolation race. The race may then be the only opportunity the spectators have to see a particular rider race against another. More likely it is a chance for the four fastest riders to determine amongst themselves just who is the best on a particular day.

For those new to, or unfamiliar with the sport, there is sometimes confusion between the Trophy Dash in a non-National meet and a Trophy Race at a National Championship meet. If the National final were named the 'A' final, then the Trophy Race could be listed as the 'B' final, for it is a race for riders who just failed to qualify for the National final.

It's all down in black and white

Above left Proof of the interest in motorcycle racing is increasing television coverage. Here Keith Jackson of ABC's *'Wide World of Sports'* program interviews winner Gary Scott at Ascot Park while promoter J. C. Agajanian looks on *(Bob Jackson)*

Above right The AMA emblem used in all advertising of sanctioned AMA race meets *(The AMA)*

Below Lined up for practise *(Bob Jackson)*

ENTRIES AND FEES

The only flat track meetings which can be pre-entered are National and Regional Championship events. All others, which constitute the majority, can be entered on race day up to 11.00 am for a day meet and 5.00pm for a night meet.

To pre-enter a National (limited to experts only) or a Regional Championship meeting, the rider pays a total of $13 (£8). $6 (£3.50) of this is an entry fee, which goes to the rider point fund and is distributed among the top finishers in any particular series. The other $7 (£4.50) is an insurance premium which, along with a promoter's contribution, pays for medical coverage (more on this later). A post or late entry received after the closing date, usually thirty days

44

It's all down in black and white

Mail Entries to American Motorcycle Assn., P. O. Box 141, Westerville, Ohio 43081
Entries must be received by April 16, 1976

OFFICIAL ENTRY BLANK

SAN JOSE
MILE NATIONAL CHAMPIONSHIP
SANTA CLARA FAIRGROUNDS, SAN JOSE, CA
SUNDAY, MAY 16, 1976

Promoted by: Bob Barkhimer Associates, Scotts Valley, CA, under the rules and sanction of the American Motorcycle Association.

25 LAP FINAL and QUALIFYING—$17,000 PURSE MONEY
(1 Mile Oval Dirt Track) EXPERT ONLY (Plus Contingencies)

The Following Events are scheduled with prizes listed:
CONTINGENCY PRIZES — AWARDS CONTINGENT ON THE USE OF THE SPONSOR'S PRODUCT & TERMS OF OFFERING

CONTINGENCY PRIZES WILL BE ANNOUNCED PRIOR TO EVENT

Race Purse

National									
1st	$2790								
2nd	1805								
3rd	1150								
4th	985								
5th	820	7th 625	9th 560	11th 490	13th 460	15th 425	17th 395	19th 360	
6th	650	8th 590	10th 525	12th 475	14th 445	16th 410	18th 375	20th 345	

Trophy Race		
1st	$ 330	
2nd	245	
3rd	215	
4th	195	
5th	165	
6th	145	7th 130 8th 115 9th 100 10th 80

4 Expert Heats 10 Laps POINT PAYING ONLY 2 Expert Semis 10 Laps POINT PAYING ONLY
$20.00 per lap to leading rider in National.
$100.00 to Fastest Time Trial.
4 Heats, 12 riders, 10 laps.
1st, 2nd, 3rd and 4th from each Heat transfer directly to National.
5th, 6th, 7th, 8th, 9th and 10th from each heat transfer to two Semi-finals.
2 Semi-finals, 12 riders each, 10 laps.
1st and 2nd from each Semi-final to the National.
3rd, 4th, 5th, 6th and 7th from each Semi-final to the Trophy Race — 10 riders - 12 laps.
National Championship, 20 riders, 25 laps.

REGISTRATION
8:00 a.m. - 11:00 a.m.
Location to be announced.

AMERICAN MOTORCYCLE ASSOCIATION

$75,000 CAMEL PRO SERIES

Camel Filters $75,000 Point Fund will include two $14,000 legs, one for the first 14 and another for the last 14 races on the schedule. A final payoff of $47,000 will be paid to the top finishers in the overall series, based on AMA National Points.

The top 10 riders in each leg of the CAMEL PRO SERIES will be paid:

1. $5,000	2. $3,000	3. $1,300	4. $900	5. $800
6. 700	7. 650	8. 600	9. 550	10. 500

At the conclusion of the 1975 CAMEL PRO SERIES, the first 10 riders overall will share in the final $47,000 fund as follows

1.$15,000	2. $9,000	3. $5,500	4. $4,000	5. $3,500
6. 3,000	7. 2,500	8. 2,000	9. 1,500	10. 1,000

ALL ENTRIES RECEIVED AFTER APR. 16, 1976, WILL BE REJECTED

I will ride a _____ Motorcycle AMA approved.

Cubic inch piston displacement _____ ;

My A.M.A. Membership No. is _____ ; expires _____ Social Security No. _____

Pro Rider No. _____

It is understood that in order to properly safeguard the contestants and avoid any possible mishap, the Director of Contests or the Committee in Charge through the authorized Referee, reserves the right to reject any entry, or entrant who in the judgment of the Referee is not fully qualified to compete in scheduled events.

I hereby agree to conform to and comply with the rules governing this contest in connection with the Competition Rules of the American Motorcycle Association, Inc., and I further agree to hold blameless the American Motorcycle Association, Inc., the Contest Committee, the Director of Contests, the promoters, owners of the premises or any of the officers, for any loss or injury to myself or property and to assume all responsibility for any loss or injury to myself or property in which I may become involved by reason of participation in this contest.

I further agree to conform to and comply with the rule that any motorcycle competing in this event can be claimed upon the payment of a stipulated price as shown in the A.M.A. Rule Book.

☐ Please check if this is a permanent change of address.

Have you read this entry blank? Answer _____

"RELEASE of LIABILITY and ASSUMPTION of RISK is contained in the APPLICATION for the COMPETITION LICENSE issued to the signer hereof"

Print Name _____

Address _____

City _____ State _____

Zip Code _____ Signed _____
Rider (must be signed in ink)

Sponsor or
Owner of machine entered _____

210-1
25-416

**MILE
SAN JOSE
5-16-76**

FOR OFFICE
USE ONLY

**Entry Fee of $13.00 Must Accompany This Entry Blank.
All Information Asked For On This Entry Must Be Supplied Or Entry Will Be Rejected
Post-Entry Fee - $25.00 + Insurance - Payable at Registration**

A National entry form *(The AMA)*

It's all down in black and white

before the meet, or at registration on race day costs the rider $25 (£15) for a National, and $15 (£9) for a Regional meet, plus the additional $7 for insurance. In both cases all of the $25 or $15 goes to the rider point fund.

At all other races which are open to experts, juniors, and novices, and for which entry blanks are not available, there is no entry fee above the insurance. However, if the purse is above $1,600 (£950) the promoter may charge the rider and mechanic a general admission fee of no more than $4 (£2.50) and $2 (£1.25) respectively.

The Camel Pro Series emblem *(The AMA)*

PRIZE MONEY

Flat track meets sanctioned by the AMA have an advertised guaranteed purse which has to be paid over to the referee in cash, prior to the racing, but this isn't to insinuate that other organizations or independent promoters don't guarantee their purses or pay out more.

National Championship races pay the biggest purses because they attract the name professionals, and hopefully, the largest crowds. Around $20,000 (£11,800) total (which includes prize money, contingency money from companies, etc.) is about average for a dirt track National, $4,000 to $5,000 (£2,350 to £2,950) of which the winner will take home.

With major sponsorship by the R.J. Reynolds Tobacco Company, AMA Grand National racing is also receiving more recognition and attention. In addition, the association is working out well for the top riders as in past seasons $75,000 (£44,100) additional to the prize money has been shared among the top riders in the title chase.

*For 1977, R.J. Reynolds has increased its series point fund to $100,000 (£60,000) and a new format for distributing that money has also been implemented. The top 14 finishers in all Camel Pro Series events will receive points according to the following schedule:

1st	-	20	4th	-	11	7th	-	8	10th - 5	13th - 2
2nd	-	16	5th	-	10	8th	-	7	11th - 4	14th - 1
3rd	-	13	6th	-	9	9th	-	6	12th - 3	

In the past seasons the Camel Pro Series point fund has been broken into three distinct payoffs - a 'first leg' covering the opening half of the season; a 'second leg' covering the final half; and an overall payoff based on final standings for the entire series. The first leg and overall payoffs remain in 1977 but the second leg payoff has been deleted:

Following is the system by which the $100,000 (£60,000) Camel Pro Series point fund will be distributed:

It's all down in black and white

First Leg Point Fund $25,000		Overall Series Point Fund $75,000	
1.	$8,000	1.	$18,000
2.	$4,000	2.	$11,000
3.	$2,500	3.	$9,000
4.	$2,100	4.	$7,000
5.	$1,800	5.	$5,000
6.	$1,600	6.	$4,500
7,	$1,500	7.	$4,000
8.	$1,300	8.	$3,500
9.	$1,200	9.	$3,000
10.	$1,100	10.	$2,500
		11.	$2,000
		12.	$1,700
		13.	$1,500
		14.	$1,300
		15.	$1,000

Over and above purse, point fund and sponsorship monies, top racers have had their incomes supplemented considerably through the AMA's Contingent Awards Program.

Thru this program, companies offer lucrative incentives to riders using particular products in competition. A total of 19 companies participated in the 1976 program and posted a record $158,625 (£93,300) for the 28 race circuit.

Start money, or appearance money as it is sometimes known, is only paid to one man at Nationals - the current National Champion. $200 (£120) will be paid to him if his appearance is guaranteed thirty days in advance, and if he attempts to qualify. No other professional

No comment *(Bob Jackson)*

It's all down in black and white

entered receives any start money; all have to rely on their ability to place well. However, promoters at all other meets can and do go the time honored route of inducing professionals with start money.

For the ordinary type AMA meet in which professionals ride, the minimum prize money can be no less than $1,200 (£720) or 30 percent of the gate, with a $900 (£530) guarantee. There is no set maximum. 70 percent of the prize money up to $2,000 (£1,200) is paid out to the experts, while the juniors receive 20 percent and the novices 10 percent. Any prize money over $2,000 (£1,200) is automatically apportioned among the experts.

Earnings in excess of $100,000 (£60,000) are now common for the current National Champion, and any expert worth his salt riding regularly can enjoy a fairly good standard of living. At the other end of the scale, prize money for juniors and novices is pale in comparison, and even with the combined junior and novice meets where the prize money is slightly more, only a few can ever hope to clear expenses. Luckily for the sport, this situation will never discourage the rider determined to succeed.

RACE RULES

The first man to take the checkered flag is the winner. Of course, everyone knows that! But did he win by fair means or foul? The only reason rules evolve in the first place is because one competitor uses unfair means or tactics to gain an advantage over another. Unfortunately, the results of 'protecting' the majority from probably one percent or less, are the compilation of ever increasing numbers of rules.

A majority of races are won or lost at the corners, and overtaking is one of those slightly gray areas where some sort of ruling is necessary. One rider overtaking another must pass on the outside, unless the leading rider has drifted out towards the fence, leaving the inside line wide open. But the responsibility of passing on the inside line lies with the overtaking rider should any mishap occur. After having overtaken on the outside, a rider must not cut over and take the inside line until two clear bike lengths have been established. Penalty for blatantly chopping up the opposition - disqualification. The overtaking rule is an effort to eliminate any unfair play, but as strategy is a big part of any racing, it could be best summed up with an example. Trying to worry an opponent into a mistake by showing him the front wheel occasionally is one thing, but jamming the wheel between his leg and the inside of the race track in an attempt to force him out is a definite no-go.

Some days nothing seems to go right *(Author)*

It's all down in black and white

Reducing frontal area by crouching down on the straights is an acceptable way of gaining two or three extra miles per hour and can be used to good advantage. However, crouching down and holding onto the fork stanchions is all that is allowed, as lying full length along the bike will result in disqualification.

Although the rules are quite specific regarding no changing of bikes or engines during a race meet, there have been (and will probably continue to be) times when the officials have turned a blind eye to exactly this. It has happened when well known experts have experienced serious engine problems prior to a final and have openly swapped machines or the irreparable engine with a good one. A casual glance in the staging area reveals the seal around the frame and engine is still intact and into the race he goes. The metal or plastic seal sometimes used during technical inspection supposedly cannot be removed except by cutting, but if patience and care are taken, it can be unfastened and reused.

The problem here is that the rules do not seem to take into consideration the spectators, who pay to see the best, expect to do so, and when all is said and done call the shots - no paying public, no professional racing. The officials in many cases understand that, hence the blind eye. After all, there are many more ways now than ever before for people to spend money on enjoyment. They don't have to come to watch motorcycle races. Perhaps this is one rule which should be updated or forgotten about in the interests of all concerned.

Tim McWhorter gives the impression of being shy when it comes to having his photograph taken
(Dan Mahony)

*THE AMA NUMBERING SYSTEM

Being Number One in any sport has a special meaning and motorcycle racing is certainly no exception. The bold black No. 1 denotes the top rider in each class and that single digit is easy to spot on the race track.

Few riders ever own a Number 1, but there are some 4,000 professional racers licensed by the AMA who strive for that goal. No two competitors carry the same number, thus the numbering of riders becomes a major task.

Different numbers are assigned to riders who compete in dirt track, road race, motocross and other forms of competition. In Grand National racing, the emphasis is placed upon earning a National number.

*Courtesy 1976 Camel Pro Series AMA Grand National Press Kit

It's all down in black and white

Just 99 riders can hold a one or two digit National number in any given season. National numbers are black on white number plates, the readily identifiable trademark of Expert rated riders. Novice riders carry red numbers on white plates and Juniors, normally the second year pros, have black numbers on yellow plates.

National Numbers are awarded by a sophisticated system that takes into consideration past performance, particularly during the previous season. Once a rider earns a National Number, he must meet certain standards each year to retain that number.

Special significance is attached to the single digit National Numbers, which are reserved for former Grand National Champions.

Riders not qualifying for a National Number are assigned a one, two or three digit number with a 'trailing' letter to signify his home district. The geographic regions represented by each letter are as follows:

A	Delaware, Pennsylvania
B	New York
C	Alabama, Georgia, North and South Carolina
D	Florida
E,R	Southern California, Hawaii
F	Ohio
G	Arizona, Colorado, Kansas, New Mexico, Oklahoma
H	Indiana
J	Idaho, Montana, Nevada, Utah, Wyoming
K	Iowa, Minnesota, Missouri, Nebraska, North and South Dakota, Wisconsin
L	Arkansas, Kentucky, Louisiana, Mississippi, Tennessee
N	Texas
P	Illinois
Q	Oregon
S	District of Columbia, Maryland, Virginia, West Virginia
T	Canada
U	Connecticut, Maine, Massachusetts, New Hampshire, New Jersey, Rhode Island, Vermont
W	Alaska, Washington
X	Michigan
Y,Z	Northern California

MECHANICS

All mechanics before being allowed into the pit area must show an official mechanic's license issued by the AMA. And yes, you guessed correctly, a license costs money, $15 (£9) to be exact. With a regular mechanic who accompanies him, many professionals have no need for the other option open to them - a John Doe license, but for those unfamiliar with the term an explanation is in order.

John Doe is a name given to designate any fictitious or real person when the name of the person is unknown. It is commonly used in the United States when illustrating how forms or documents should be filled out, and can be used in any legal transaction or proceedings. The rider purchases a license at $10 (£6) then passes it around to whoever will accompany him as a mechanic.

Over the years the AMA has done its share in trying to present motorcycle racing as a respectable sport to a public bombarded with sensationalism and bad publicity from ill-informed sources. In furtherance of this goal, a code of dress for mechanics was enacted many years ago and although not as strictly enforced as it has been in the past, either white coveralls, or white pants and shirt are required to be worn. While white may not be the most practical color for a mechanic, the dress code seems a concept worth hanging onto in the still continuing battle for respectability.

It's all down in black and white

The front straight of a half mile track as riders see it coming off the corner *(Bob Jackson)*

CLAIMING RULE

In AMA racing, any competitor in the same event and class may lay claim to either of the first three machines across the finish line. The rule originated primarily as a deterrent to factory teams against using anything other than approved parts and machinery. Special internal parts may not be able to be seen, but riders generally are not fooled, and there is always the grapevine along which information passes.

In recent years the rule has been updated to allow for increased costs and, whereas the complete motorcycle was purchased previously, now only the complete engine and transmission, ignition system and carburetors are claimable. The price for a 750cc engine is $3,500 (£2,100) and for a 250cc, $2,500 (£1,500). Cash, certified check, or bank draft must accompany the claim, which must be made to the referee no later than thirty minutes after the completion of the event.

Claiming another rider's machine is unique to American racing and considered slightly bizarre by enthusiasts in other countries. For instance, in European road racing the spectators favor seeing the exotic machinery only a handful of manufacturers can produce, and GP racing tends to be a battle between the few companies who are prepared to shell out vast amounts of money. It's just a whole different approach and any arguments for and against either concept can be of no value, for the two sides will never see eye to eye.

OFFENSES – APPEALS – REINSTATEMENTS – PROTESTS

The AMA splits this section of the rule book into the four parts of the heading and while there is no intention of boring the reader with the various offenses, there are a couple of paragraphs worth mentioning.

When first reading thru these rules, it appears the referee and officials have the power of life and death over the riders, but luckily this is not the case. Fifty riders signing a petition can bring a referee to task and any charges are investigated by a board appointed by the president of the AMA.

The list of offenses covers the spectrum from bribes to fixing races, but the one liner which seems to jump off the page (probably because it contains so few words and immediately catches the eye) refers to attacks on AMA officials. No doubt at some time or another a referee has been punched in the mouth (and maybe even deserved it) but why does this rule

It's all down in black and white

instantly bring to mind a comic picture. Two men, one walking quickly and obviously annoyed, the other with a bloody nose desparately trying to keep up, while leafing thru the rule book for the offense. While no one is advocating 'punch ups', perhaps rules can be taken too far.

Appeals and reinstatements are long winded affairs, involving appeal boards, and as the majority of riders never even get as far as talking to the referee (let alone attacking him), no purpose can be gained from discussing them here.

Protests tend to leave a nasty taste in the mouth but they are justifiable if someone 'done you wrong'. Although it doesn't happen often, any rider may protest the piston displacement of another's machine, in writing to the referee at a cost of $50 (£30) for a National Championship and $25 (£15) all other meets. If, after the engine has been measured, it is regulation size, the protested rider receives the money. The other side of the coin, an oversize engine, results in a suspension and a fine with the money being returned to its original owner.

OFFICIALS

It takes a lot of people to run a motorcycle race. The list runs down from referee, starter, clerk of the course, headscorer, timer, judges and umpires, pit steward, scrutineer, and starting line observer. All have their respective jobs and while some are overly officious, others are lax; some are liked and some disliked, but they all share a common bond with the riders and spectators - a more than passing interest in motorcycles and racing. A good many are old (?) retired racers, who do not wish to lose their ties with the sport, but to many officialdom appears like an ogre which grows larger with every passing year. Motorcycle racing, as with any sport, needs its officials, and all of us should remember these people are friends not enemies, there to help, not hinder.

The starter needs a big bag in which to carry around all his flags *(Author)*

PROMOTERS

The professional promoter of any motorcycle event (lets not be squeamish about this) is trying to make money and obviously thinks he can, otherwise he'd be doing something else. Promoting is just like any other business. It incurs expenses in trying to make money but expenses eat away at the bottom line especially if the spectators don't turn up as they should. And whereas certain expenses can be trimmed, others regarding the safety of the riders cannot, for safety is the sole responsibility of the promoter. Two ambulances with an oxygen supply, plus a doctor at National meets, fire extinguishers, marshals, hay bales and numerous other things must all be provided at the promoter's expense.

Now the tears may not be welling up in your eyes at the plight of the promoter, but it is worth remembering no profit could be the end of professional racing. So riders and spectators, support motorcycle racing by supporting your local promoter - especially if he's a good one.

It's all down in black and white

Effective January 1, 1976, all machines were required to be muffled in the interests of better public relations. More development is reducing the mufflers to a more acceptable size *(Bob Jackson)*

INSURANCE

Motorcycle racing is dangerous. Riders do sometimes get hurt, requiring help or hospitalization, and if there is one thing those unfamiliar with the US know, it is that medical attention in this country costs money. With no governmental health plan existing whereby medical care is dispensed virtually free of charge, the majority of people are covered by private insurance companies. As this is a book about racing, there is no intention to debate the pros and cons of the system, except that it is mentioned with reference to the AMA's rider participation insurance program. For the pure professional, the AMA group insurance is probably the only game in town as the premiums for an individual medical policy would literally cost an arm and a leg.

The AMA insurance has no deductible, the AMA (not the insurance company or the rider) pays 100% of the first $100 (£60) of medical expenses. For any expenses in excess of $100 up to $10,000 (£6,000) the insurance company pays 75%, the rider 25%.

Should the rider be prevented from engaging in his occupation, a weekly disability payment of $30 (£18) is paid, beginning the second week for a period of thirteen weeks.

Accidental death and loss of limbs is covered with a one time payment ranging from $5,000 (£3,000) down to $1,250 (£735).

Many novice, junior, and even part-time expert riders who hold down full-time jobs are usually covered by a group medical insurance plan partially paid for by themselves and partially by their employers. In most instances, should a racing accident occur, this group policy also covers a percentage of expenses incurred for medical attention. In effect the AMA insurance pays first, the group policy pays second, with the rider picking up the tab for the remainder, if there is any.

It's all down in black and white

*OFFICIAL AMA FLAGS

Flags are an important part of any racing and the following measuring 30 in by 30 in are used.

Green	Start of the race
White	One lap to go to finish of race
Yellow	Danger on the track
Red	Stopping race for emergency situation
Yellow With Red Stripes	(Three 2 in red stripes running perpendicular to staff). There is oil on the track beyond this flag
Black With White Border	(1 in white border). Disqualification of an individual rider, report to the referee
Light Blue	Move over, another rider trying to pass
White With Red Cross	(Cross 20 in by 20 in by 6 in wide). Ambulance flag, indicating an ambulance is out on the track. All safety cornermen are issued with a red cross flag. The flag is displayed by the safety official to signal only when an ambulance is needed
Black And White Checkered	(Checks 5 in by 5 in). Finish, end of race

*Courtesy 1976 AMA Professional Dirt Track Competition Rule Book

4 Not your average street bike

THE 750CC GRAND NATIONAL MACHINES ARE BIG GUTSY MONSTERS BUT THE CHANCES ARE YOU WILL NEVER SEE ONE FOR SALE AT THE LOCAL MOTORCYCLE STORE. WHILE LIMITED NUMBERS OF OVER-THE-COUNTER RACE MACHINES ARE AVAILABLE FOR BOTH THE HEAVY-WEIGHT AND LIGHTWEIGHT CLASSES, FLAT TRACK RACING IS AT PRESENT A SPORT IN WHICH MACHINES BUILT FROM SCRATCH OUT-NUMBER THE COMMERCIALLY AVAILABLE PRODUCTS.

It is no surprise to those who actively follow the sport that Harley-Davidson is the sole company manufacturing 750cc over-the-counter flat track machines. In fact, in many instances Harley engines in either Harley or other makes of frames constitute the bulk of the entry. The reason - there are relatively few other 750cc twin cylinder engines available which are, or can be made competitive. One manufacturer - Yamaha - does actively support the sport through its one factory rider - Kenny Roberts - though does not, probably for economic reasons, build and sell production racing machines. Triumphs, once very competitive, and an occasional Norton and BSA make up the rest of the field, but these, like any Yamahas, are built by riders or owners.

On some tracks the English and Japanese engines are still a force to be reckoned with, and this seems a suitable time to pay tribute to the tuners and owners who continue to race them for no other reason than that they enjoy the challenge of trying to beat off the Harley-Davidson onslaught. In the majority of cases, men such as Ron Wood with his Nortons, Gary Davis, Bill Kennedy and Jack Hateley with their Triumphs, and Shell Thuet with his Yamahas, spend vast amounts of money and time with next to no chance of seeing any return for it. They persevere, nevertheless, and should be recognized for their contribution, especially as the majority of us take delight in cheering on the underdog.

With so few engines in use for the heavyweight division, it might appear that the racing, generally a Harley-Davidson benefit, is consequently unexciting to watch. Happily, attendance figures don't bear this out, for they are increasing year by year, proving that the racing is better than it has ever been. Admittedly, part of the excitment has always been the battles between different manufacturers. In effect two races take place - one rider against another, and one make of machine against another. At present there is no real contest among the manu-facturers on the flat tracks, but while Harley-Davidsons invariably fill the top spots, one never knows which rider will win until the checkered flag comes out.

As with all limited production racing bikes (both 750 and 250cc) the question of availability always crops up. Can anyone with the money buy one? The answer - yes and no. In general, a certain amount are made to cover existing orders and then that's it until the next batch. A rider who wants one will have made sure his order was in well ahead of time.

The subject of race engines always brings up horsepower figures, and as they are, and always will be, an area of controversy, some information about the figures about to be given is in order.

Not your average street bike

On more than one occasion during the 1976 season this Ron Wood-owned Norton had British bike enthusiasts in the stands on their feet yelling encouragement to rider Alex Jorgensen *(Bob Jackson)*

All were obtained by the same person, on a regularly calibrated dynamometer which measures horsepower at the rear wheel sprocket, hence the performance of any one engine can be compared directly against another.

Let us then examine the one production race bike available for experts, tuning and alternative engines used, followed by the lightweight class, and finally the specialty manufacturers who supply the hardware for building a machine.

HARLEY-DAVIDSON XR750

There is little doubt that the XR750 is the machine of the moment. The engine churns out a lot of horsepower which currently no other twin can match, but more, it is power that can be put to the ground and used. The only opposition of late (on mile tracks) has been the four cylinder TZ750 Yamaha two-stroke, a road race engine in a flat track frame. The bike, however, was banned along with other engines with more than two cylinders.

The V-twin has been a part of American motorcycling since the earliest days, and contrary to popular belief, the engines did not grow in displacement because there was a lack of design expertise to obtain similar power from smaller engines. The engines have always been large, with the V-twin the neatest package which could produce a reasonably compact, durable, and extremely powerful machine. Most of all the buying public liked and accepted the configuration much as riders in other countries preferred the vertical twin.

There is nothing startling or unconventional about the XR750, it is just a basically well designed 'bullet proof' engine. But it wasn't always so. When introduced in the early seventies, the engine was not all that powerful and not particularly reliable. The task of bringing the

Harley-Davidson XR750 *(Author)*

HARLEY-DAVIDSON XR750

ENGINE

Type	V-twin overhead valve four stroke
Displacement	749cc
Bore x Stroke	79.4 x 75.7 mm
Horsepower	71-73 (at rear wheel sprocket)
Ignition Type	Fairbanks-Morse magneto
Carburetors	38 mm Mikuni
Air Filters	K & N fabric

DRIVETRAIN

Gearbox	4 speed
Primary/Ratio	3/8 in Triple chain/various
Secondary/Ratio	5/8 in Single row chain/various
Clutch	Multiple plates - dry

CHASSIS AND SUSPENSION

Head Angle	26 degrees ± 30'
Trail	3.437 in
Front Suspension	Ceriani. Springs with hydraulic dampening
Rear Suspension	Swing arm with Girling shocks
Rear Brake	Disk. Manufactured in USA
Front Tire	3.50 or 4.00 x 19 in diameter
Rear Tire	4.00 x 19 in diameter

GENERAL DETAILS

Wheelbase	56.75 in max
Seat Height	31 in
Gas Tank Capacity	2.5 US Gallons
Oil Tank Capacity	2.75 US Qts
Dry Weight	310 lb approx.

Not your average street bike

Dick O'Brien, Harley-Davidson's Race Director, the man behind the successful XR750 engine *(Author)*

engine up to scratch has not been the pouring of thousands upon thousands of 'horsepower dollars' into the project. Rather it has been the slow tedious time consuming development work of a few people who have nursed the XR750 along its 'learning curve'. Race Director Dick O'Brien, Clyde Denzer, Cyril 'Babe' DeMay, and Ron Alexander are the four men to whom the vast majority of the credit must go, for over the last few years they have worked laboriously at upping the power and increasing the reliability. Their work should not go unsung.

From the factory an XR will pump out between 71 and 73 horsepower, but with extra work this figure has gone as high as 88.8 horsepower, with no loss of reliability. In fact, at the higher figure the engine is even 'happier' and will last through one half season of racing before any major work need be done.

If there is a secret to the XR750's success on the dirt tracks, it is in the heavy flywheels which give excellent traction when accelerating out of corners and enables 'tall' gearing to be pulled down the straights. Successful engines in American dirt track racing, whether twin or single, have always followed this formula, and riders and tuners have been quick to pick up on basically well designed engines with heavy flywheels. The BSA Gold Star is a classic example. It is still remembered and revered, and long after production was halted at Small Heath, the engine was being developed and raced on American tracks.

In recent years the XR750 has achieved the enviable position of being the most powerful and reliable engine in use on the dirt tracks *(Author)*

Not your average street bike

Belying its appearance of looking massively heavy, the XR750 weighs approximately 310 lb dry. Admittedly this may seem a lot when compared to a 250cc machine, but the power to weight ratio of the XR beats that of any smaller machine. Nor is it nearing the end of its development or life. There is still horsepower to be found in the engine, with two or three extra 'ponies' appearing every year - which confounds anyone who asks, 'Just how much faster can they go?'

Until either the displacement rules are changed, different engine configurations allowed, or a twin as reliable and as powerful comes along, the XR750 will remain the King of the hill.

The Gentlemanly Art Of Tuning Engines

In the industrial section of San Fernando Road in Glendale, California, stands a building, the glass doors of which bear only a name - C.R. Axtell. There is no indication of who the company is or what it does, but the building is something of a Mecca for flat track racers. And the initials C.R. or more usually just 'Ax' are enough for many to identify the man whose name appears on the door. C.R. Axtell is a tuner with a reputation that stretches from Japan to Europe. His work is legendary among American racers and hardly a day goes by without someone dropping in for advice, more horsepower, or just a chat with him or his two dedicated employees, Mike Libby and Bob Bell.

Over the years many machines have been bolted down to Ax's dyno (horsepower figures from which appear in this text) and he will tell you quite openly that there is only one engine for the serious expert - a Harley XR750. It requires less tuning work than any other engine, can produce a lot more horsepower, and as was mentioned previously, lasts a lot longer into the bargain.

C. R. (Ax) Axtell the well known tuner (at right) at work on his dyno while his friend Ron Wood, owner of the 80hp Norton being measured, looks on *(Author)*

Experimentation with exhaust and inlet systems play a large part in extracting more power from the Harley beast. In addition, Mert Lawwill or Sifton camshafts, along with larger inlet valves and ports, and maybe larger exhaust valves, are fitted. Basically, just these few parts, plus ignition timing and carburetion tuning, are all that are required to take an XR750 engine up to almost 90 horsepower. Mert's own machine is the 88.8 horsepower model briefly mentioned earlier, and at present the machine is still running as reliably and as competitively as ever.

Compare this to a Triumph twin, which requires far more work to reach 70 horsepower at which it will not last for any great length of time. One of the basic problems with the

Not your average street bike

Axtell's machine shop is well equipped to make many of the high performance parts installed in customer's engines *(Author)*

Triumph design has been the lack of a center main bearing without which the increased power and out of balance forces in the center flywheel destroy the crankshaft. With a balance factor of 80%, plus weight removed from the center flywheel and added to the outer counter-weights, the engine can be made to 'live' a little longer, but the weak link of no center main bearing still remains.

A few years ago THE engine to use. Triumphs nevertheless are still competitive on some tracks, and in TT racing *(Bob Jackson)*

Not your average street bike

Kenny Robert's 750cc overhead cam factory Yamaha twin *(Author)*

The other requirements are: new intake and exhaust valves plus lightened rockers in the re-worked head, valve guides, S & W springs, Hepolite pistons, (according to Axtell the best available), camshaft and Amal GP or Dellorto carburetors.

Before the engine is assembled, the oiling system is worked over in an effort to dry up the crankcase, the clutch balanced, and the transmission plus some other parts hard chromed for longer life. Finally, with the Lucas ignition replaced by a total loss system, the engine pumps out a fair amount of horsepower.

Magnafluxing, zyglo inspection and x-raying for cracks, one of the largest single expenses of Axtell's business, is performed on parts before and after work is done. As he points out, 'What is the good of spending a nickel on a part if it isn't worth a nickel to start with.'

Of the remaining British twins still in use, the Norton with considerable work can be made competitive at around 80 horsepower. Unfortunately with the demise of the industry and subsequent lack of parts, things don't look bright for the riders of British twins in 1977.

At present the 750cc Yamaha four stroke twin, which is really a bored out 650, is the only other popular twin currently being used, and a few are within striking distance of the best Harleys on some of the longer tracks. Typical of Japanese design is the lack of weight in the flywheel, which coupled with a wide crankshaft, puts the engine at a disadvantage for this type of racing.

Some of the problems with the engine have been in the cylinder head. The engine does not breathe as well as it should, and in an effort to become competitive with the best Harley-Davidsons, the factory produced new, better designed cylinder heads. The factory engines, though turning out more horsepower than ever before, were still in the development stage throughout most of the '76 season, but they did show there was potential for even more power which should appear this year.

Limited to the existing cylinder head, Axtell has also had considerable success in extracting power from the Yamaha engine. By making new connecting rods, the bottom ends of which were thickened considerably, he succeeded in adding weight to the crankshaft. This weight was in addition to that added to the flywheels themselves. Before starting the project, Axtell had decided to test a few theories of his own and designed, and had cast his own pistons. Coupled with the more usual tuning work, the results were engines giving out slightly in excess of 79 horsepower.

Not your average street bike

With redesigned cylinder heads for the '76 season the Yamaha put out more power than ever before, with the potential for even more *(Author)*

THE LIGHTWEIGHTS

In the 250cc class, the machines used on short tracks and by novices, the situation is somewhat different to that of the 750cc class. The recent rule change limiting everyone to a 250cc single cylinder engine has attracted some new manufacturers and an upsurge in racing is expected. Previously only one company - Bultaco - offered a 250cc machine.

Some new quarter liter production race machines are now becoming available, though at time of writing very little information other than what appears on the specificaton sheets is known about them. Red Line Engineering, a well known frame manufacturer in Northridge, California, has produced a batch of complete machines with brand new KTM and Can-Am engines, which are currently being marketed by the company as Champion-KTM's and Champion Can-Am's. The Ossa Parts and Service Corporation have also thrown their hat into the ring with a number of American-framed Ossa two-strokes, and an Italian engined Harley-Davidson ridden on the short tracks in 1976 by Jay Springsteen is almost certainly a prelude to a production bike. Other manufacturers and distributors will no doubt follow this lead in the future.

With everyone starting from scratch, any evaluation of existing individual engines would be an injustice until all have been through at least one season's racing to find any inherent weak points. Even the established 250cc Bultaco Astro has undergone a personality change by reason of bore and stroke modifications, which effectively makes it a different engine to the one previously raced.

Not your average street bike

Champion-KTM

CHAMPION-KTM
ENGINE
Type	Single cylinder piston ported two stroke
Displacement	245.54cc
Bore x Stroke	71 x 62 mm
Horsepower	38 (manufacturers stated figure, take off point unknown)
Ignition Type	Electronic
Carburetor	36 mm Bing
Air Filter	K & N fabric

DRIVETRAIN
Gearbox	6 speed
Primary/Ratio	Geardrive/3.00 (25/75)
Secondary/Ratio	530 Single row Denselube chain/not available
Clutch	Multiple plates in oil

CHASSIS AND SUSPENSION
Frame	4130 Chromoly, heli-arc welded, nickel plated
Head Angle	25½ degrees
Front Suspension	Ceriani. Springs with hydraulic dampening
Rear Suspension	Swing arm with S & W shocks
Rear Brake	Kosman disk with Grimeca hydraulics
Front Tire	4.00 x 19 in diameter Goodyear Eagle D T
Rear Tire	4.00 x 19 in diameter Goodyear Eagle D T

GENERAL DETAILS
Wheelbase	53.5 - 55.5 in
Seat Height	30 in
Gas Tank Capacity	1.5 US Gallons
Dry Weight	Not available

Not your average street bike

Ossa ST-1

OSSA ST-1

ENGINE

Type	Single cylinder piston ported two stroke
Displacement	244.35cc
Bore x Stroke	72 x 60 mm
Horsepower	Not available
Ignition Type	Electronic
Carburetor	34 mm
Air Filter	K & N fabric

DRIVETRAIN

Gearbox	5 Speed
Primary/Ratio	3/8 in Duplex chain/2.26 (15/34)
Secondary/Ratio	520 Single row Full Bore chain/5.00 (12/60)
Clutch	Multiple plates in oil

CHASSIS AND SUSPENSION

Frame	4130 Chromoly, heli-arc welded, nickel plated
Head Angle	25½ degrees
Front Suspension	Springs with hydraulic dampening
Rear Suspension	Swing arm with 5 way adjustable shocks
Rear Brake	Disk. Manufactured in USA
Front Tire	3.50 x 19 in diameter Full Bore
Rear Tire	4.00 x 19 in diameter Full Bore

GENERAL DETAILS

Wheelbase	52.5 - 55 in
Seat Height	30 in
Gas Tank Capacity	1.5 US Gallons
Dry Weight	195 lb approx.

Not your average street bike

Champion-Can-Am

CHAMPION-CAN-AM
ENGINE
Type	Single cylinder rotary valve two stroke
Displacement	247.37cc
Bore x Stroke	74 x 57.5 mm
Horsepower	37 (manufacturers stated figure, take off point unknown)
Ignition Type	Bosch capacitor discharge
Carburetor	32 mm
Air Filter	K & N fabric

DRIVETRAIN
Gearbox	5 Speed
Primary/Ratio	Geardrive/2.91 (23/67)
Secondary/Ratio	5/8 in Single row Denselube chain/not available
Clutch	Multiple plates in oil

CHASSIS AND SUSPENSION
Frame	4130 Chromoly, heli-arc welded, nickel plated
Head Angle	25½ degrees
Front Suspension	Ceriani. Springs with hydraulic dampening
Rear Suspension	Swing arm with S & W shocks
Rear Brake	Kosman disk with Grimeca hydraulics
Front Tire	4.00 x 19 in diameter Goodyear Eagle D T
Rear Tire	4.00 x 19 in diameter Goodyear Eagle D T

GENERAL DETAILS
Wheelbase	53.5 - 55.5 in
Seat Height	30 in
Gas Tank Capacity	1.5 US Gallons
Dry Weight	192 lb approx.

Not your average street bike

Bultaco Astro

BULTACO ASTRO
ENGINE
Type	Single cylinder piston ported two stroke
Displacement	244.29cc
Bore x Stroke	70 x 64 mm
Horsepower	38 (manufacturers stated figure, take off point unknown)
Ignition Type	Electronic
Carburetor	36 mm Bing
Air Filter	Washable foam

DRIVETRAIN
Gearbox	5 Speed
Primary/Ratio	3/8 in Duplex chain/2.375 (16/38)
Secondary/Ratio	5/8 in Single row Joresa chain/4.75 (12/57)
Clutch	Multiple plates in oil

CHASSIS AND SUSPENSION
Front Suspension	Bultaco design and manufacture. Springs with hydraulic dampening
Rear Suspension	Swing arm with Betor shocks
Rear Brake	Disk. Manufactured in USA
Front Tire	3.50 x 19 in diameter
Rear Tire	3.50 x 19 in diameter

GENERAL DETAILS
Wheelbase	54.5 in
Seat Height	31.4 in
Gas Tank Capacity	1.32 US Gallons
Dry Weight	191 lb approx.

Not your average street bike

BULTACO ASTRO

The Astro, as it is known today, is the result of development by American riders: Mike Kidd, Roger Crump, and Guy McClure. A complete machine prepared by Kidd was sent to Spain with instructions from Virginia Beach to 'build it just like that'. Having little more than rudimentary knowledge of this arm of the sport (why should they, there is no flat tracking in Spain) the factory followed the instructions to the letter, producing a batch of production models with bent right side footpegs. The bent original had been the result of a complete season's racing!

The engine is a simple piston ported two-stroke, a design Bultaco has stuck with through thick and thin, even when the rotary valve was touted as the wave of the future. The oversquare engine is fed by a large 36mm Bing carburetor which, coupled to the porting and resonant effect of the exhaust system, results in a quoted horsepower output of 38.

With the exception of the US-made disk brake, plus items such as tires and carburetor, the machine is made entirely in Spain. Such is the quality that it requires little or no replacement of parts more acceptable to the American rider. Even the reversible rear hub is universal in that other than Bultaco sprockets can be used.

That the Astro has been successful for Bultaco there is little doubt. The parent company has not overridden the advice of the American riders in favor of their own ideas of how things should be done, consequently everyone is happy with the machine. And the three riders involved in the development are impressed enough with the results to contribute still to the machine's furthering development.

Building a machine

Ask the question why someone should go to the trouble of building his own machine, and the answers will be as diverse as the builders themselves. Some will say they enjoy the challenge, others will point out that with the limited choice and availability of production models the task is unavoidable, while still yet others believe they can build a machine, which because it contains no compromises, will be superior in every way to anything currently available. In general, the reason for the specialty manufacturer's existance is that they fill a void motorcycle manufacturers, by reason of economics or lack of expertise, do not want to, or are unwilling to fill.

Besides the engine, the frame is probably the most expensive item on the shopping list. Of the existing frame manufacturers, Red Line Engineering, Trackmaster, C & J Precision Products and Kennedy all build their frames of chromoly tubing, while K-R Racing Specialities (Kenny Roberts) use mild steel. Immensely stronger and lighter than mild steel, chromoly is nevertheless expensive, tricky to weld, and sometimes difficult to repair. Roberts' argument is that a correctly designed mild steel frame is up to the job, easily repairable and just as importantly, costs less than a chromoly counterpart. Whichever choice is made, the builder is assured of a high standard of quality, with each joint neatly heli-arc welded.

Around a 26 degree head angle produces quick and responsive steering, although the position of the engine in the frame and length of the swing arm are of equal importance. The weight has to be proportioned to ensure sufficient bite at the rear tire, while maintaining a heavy enough front end which doesn't 'push' through corners.

The more normal swing arm and almost vertical rear shocks may seem old hat compared to motocross standards, but this set-up will probably endure, as there is really no need for longer travel. Some riders are currently experimenting with monoshock type rear ends, not to gain more travel, but in an effort to get even more traction.

Not your average street bike

The majority of speciality manufacturers are small independent businessmen enthusiasts. Here Lynn Kastan and Paul Hunt of Red Line Engineering give a completed frame a final once over *(Author)*

Apart from the head angle, the most radical departure from conventional frames is in the footpeg positioning. The right footpeg (when sitting on the machine) is about on a level with the bottom frame rail, and 2 in to 3 in further back towards the swing arm pivot. In this position the rider can exert tremendous leverage with his leg and boot, to put the motor-cycle into the broadsliding attitude. The left footpeg is positioned even further back than the right, and higher. In this position the outstretched foot automatically 'clicks' into place at the exit of the corner, and as importantly it ensures there is no chance of the peg digging in the ground when keeled over.

Not your average street bike

Uncompromising design and workmanship make the kit frame a thing of beauty
(Dan Mahony)

In the suspension department one set of front forks - Ceriani - is preferred above all others. The forks with their internal springs and excellent dampening have been the pattern for practically every other fork now in use. In addition to being extremely light in weight, the well engineered road race triple clamps used cock the front wheel out just slightly to give 3.5 in of trail. This combination has been found the best over the years, and is probably used by ninety percent of all riders.

One other major consideration for using Ceriani forks is that the stanchions will bend in hard crashes! This is a desirable feature as riders who used forks made of exotic materials found that although the forks survived a hard shock, the frame did not. The force of crashing simply passed through the unbendable forks to the next most easily bendable object - the frame. And it doesn't take a degree in economics to understand that replacing the forks is considerably cheaper than replacing the frame.

250cc machines are also fitted with the same 'heavyweight' forks mainly because flexing problems occur with smaller models. The frame geometry (26 degrees head angle, 3.5 in of trail) also remains constant for the smaller class as these dimensions give the best results.

Red Wing and S & W shock absorbers, two of the many choices available for springing the rear end (Red Wing - Author)

Not your average street bike

To control the rear suspension, S & W, Girling, Koni, Red Wing and Boge are among the most widely used shock absorbers. In addition, there are lesser known makes including some Japanese units, which can be seen occasionally. With no one make of shock absorber more technically outstanding than any other for this type of racing, selection is merely a matter of personal preference.

Before getting to the most popular wheels used, some background information on tires is necessary, for both are interrelated. Ever since riders have been looking for the slight edge which could help them win a race, there has been no one tire which could be used on a majority of race tracks. Different tires are used to suit the various surfaces and it is not unusual to swap wheels throughout the day as the track surface changes or deteriorates. Under certain conditions the rear tires wear rapidly and will not last through a day's racing. Where only the leading edge of the tire wears away, the wheel can be removed, the sprocket attached to the other side of the hub, and a fresh edge offered to the ground. The reversible wheel has long been a feature of flat track racing. When finally both edges have been rounded off, a razor blade is brought out and fresh edges cut into the tire.

In the space of a year's racing this scene has changed somewhat for mile tracks.

To try and combat the traction problems the Yamaha team experienced with the TZ750 flat track machine, Goodyear experimented with various combinations of tread patterns and rubber compounds. Early efforts were not too successful, but development continued and the result has been a tire, the D/TII, which has made obsolete the majority of tires in current use on mile tracks. The D/TII rear tire (one is also available for the front wheel) gives more 'side-bite' when power sliding through corners, and 'hooks up' to the ground quicker, coming off corners. The results have been startling - lower lap times by as much as a second on mile tracks. Just as importantly the rear tire will last through a day's racing at the National level.

Nor is this the end of the story for a new tire for use on half mile tracks, made with different compounds to that of the D/TII, will possibly be produced during 1977.

Though Goodyear D/T II tires have reduced the need for different kinds of tires on the vast majority of mile tracks, until recently, varying types (admittedly not as many as shown here) were necessary for constantly changing track surfaces. At present, different types of tires are still required for half mile tracks *(Bob Jackson)*

When the tire supply got low, a razor blade would be brought out to straighten up the rounded off edges of the tread *(Bob Jackson)*

Above left A Barnes hub. Two types are available: large and small flanged. This large flanged model is primarily for rear wheel use but it can be used at the front *(Author)*

Above right The latest Morris cast wheels on which riders are mounting the new Goodyear D/T II tires *(Author)*

Below left The optional disc brake which the majority of top professionals use only in emergency situations *(Author)*

Below right The hydraulic master cylinder is connected to the brake lever through a simple linkage. The hose disappearing through the number plate is a breather *(Author)*

Above left Although K & N filters fitted to Harley-Davidsons might appear cumbersome they are rubber mounted and move under pressure from the rider's leg *(Author)*

Above right Gas tanks can usually be purchased with the frame. This unusual but neat looking tank is a Champion design *(Bob Jackson)*

Below left An immaculate fiber glass gas tank for Harley-Davidson's is available from Don Vesco Products *(Author)*

Below right Numerous handlebar bends are available to suit all tastes

(Bob Jackson)

Not your average street bike

Up until the Goodyear D/TII tires became available, spoked wheels were used universally. Laced to either Barnes, Kosman or Kennedy hubs they have, and still do, give good service. Unfortunately, the lack of availability of a spoked rim wider than WM4 on which to mount a D/TII rear tire has shifted the emphasis to a cast wheel with a WM6 rim. Although the tire works on a WM4 spoked wheel, to use its full potential the wider rim is advisable in order to put as much tread as possible in contact with the ground. Enter Morris cast aluminum wheels, which fit all the necessary requirements: WM6 rim, reversible, lightweight, etc. And for the more weight conscious there is even a magnesium version.

There is a concern among some followers of the sport that the additional expense for more wheels and tires puts those who can least afford them at a disadvantage. True, the equipment is more expensive and no argument, however good, can alter the fact. But is the picture as bad as it is painted? Existing spoked wheels can still be used, and because the tires last longer than any others used, this helps offset the increased price.

One of the more popular disk brakes fitted to machines is an hydraulic unit manufactured by Hurst Airheart, but there are other types used which are as good, and in the minds of some, much better. The disk, like the rear sprocket, is held in place on the rear wheel with a quick release locking ring, and the caliper is bolted below the swing arm. The slim master cylinder is attached directly to the frame in the area of the swing arm pivot, and coupled through a simple linkage to the brake lever.

Where air filters are concerned, the choice has to be a fabric type made by K & N Engineering. Foam filters have been tried but the majority dislike them for as the dirt builds up it begins to clog the tunnels in the foam, affecting the element's breathing capacity. Dust and dirt will not, however, clog a K & N filter, for it remains on the outside of the element and is utilized in the filtering action. The corrugated design also permits more surface area for breathing than does any other filter of similar dimensions. K & N filters are available for a host of engines, from the long variety used on Harley-Davidsons to the more usual pancake types used on many 250s.

Except for the chain, the majority of other items necessary to complete the motorcycle are, like shock absorbers, whatever the rider prefers. For many years Renolds chain held the limelight, but other manufacturers have since entered the market and currently Diamond chain is held in high esteem for flat tracking.

Gas tanks and seats can as a rule be purchased with the frame, or separately, as preferred. Alloy, fiberglass, and plastic are all acceptable gas tank materials and the smaller, under two gallon types, attach quite satisfactorily to the frame with a universal center bolt mounting.

Cables, controls, number plates, handlebars with differing bends, throttles, and all the small things that go into the building of a motorcycle, such as cable ties and plastic hose, are all items available from the manufacturers or motorcycle stores.

Following is a list of flat track machine manufacturers, and manufacturers or distributors of cycle parts and equipment for, or used on, flat track machines. The list is by no means complete but these are some of the products mentioned in the text of the previous chapter. Some items are distributed by other companies in various areas of the country.

Motorcycle Manufacturers
Harley-Davidson Motor Co., Inc.
3700 W. Juneau
Milwaukee, Wis. 53201
Tel: (414)-342-4680

Bultaco International Ltd.
5447 Greenwich Road
Virginia Beach, Va. 23462
Tel: (804)-499-8501

Not your average street bike

Ossa Parts and Service Corp.
PO Box 36,
Schenectady, NY. 12301
Tel: (518)-372-4726

Red Line Engineering
18257 Parthenia
Northridge,
California 91325
Tel: (213)-886-1728

Frame Manufacturers
Red Line Engineering *(Champion frames)*
18257 Parthenia
Northridge,
Calif. 91325
Tel: (213)-886-1728

C & J Precision Products
3873 S. Main Street
Santa Ana, Calif. 92707
Tel: (714)-540-7350

Trackmaster Racing Frames
18548 Parthenia
Northridge, Calif. 91324
Tel: (213)-349-9487

K-R Racing Specialties
9600 Pioneer Avenue,
Oakdale, Calif. 95361
Tel: (209)-847-2572

Kennedy Manufacturing and Distributing *(Star frames)*
4363 S. Seneca
Wichita, Kansas. 67217
Tel: (316)-522-3414

Front Forks
Ceriani   Accessory Distributors Inc.
                  175 Fair Street
                  Palisades Park, NJ. 07658
                  Tel: (201)-947-8200

Rear Shocks
S & W   S & W Engineered Products
                  12268 Woodruff Avenue
                  Downey, Calif. 90241
                  Tel: (213)-869-9560

Koni   Bikoni Ltd.
                  150 Green Street
                  Hackensack, NJ. 07601
                  Tel: (201)-489-0404

Red Wing	Marubeni American Corp. 200 Park Avenue New York, NY 10017 Tel: (212)-973-8937
Girling	Lucas Industries N. America Inc. 2 Northfield Plaza Troy, Mich. 48084 Tel: (313)-879-1920

Wheels

Barnes	Alloy Sprocket Specialties 10146 Stagg Street Sun Valley, Calif. 91352 Tel: (213)-767-6984
Morris	Morris Industries 2901 W. Garry Avenue Santa Ana, Calif. 92704 Tel: (714)-540-5206
Kosman	Kosman Specialties 340 Fell Street San Francisco, Calif. 91402 Tel: (415)-861-4262
Kennedy	Kennedy Manufacturing and Distributing 4363 S. Seneca Wichita, Kansas. 67217 Tel: (316)-522-3414

Tires

Goodyear Tire & Rubber Co.
1144 E. Market Street
Akron, Ohio. 44316
Tel: (216)-794-2391

Carlisle Tire & Rubber Co.
Box 99
Carlisle, Pa. 17013
Tel: (717)-249-1000

Pirelli Tire Corp.
600 Third Avenue
New York, NY 10016
Tel: (212)-490-1300

Dunlop Tire & Rubber Corp.
Box 1109
Buffalo, NY 14213
Tel: (716)-877-2200

Headers

Jardine	Jardine Headers 7142 Belgrave Avenue Garden Grove, Calif. 92641 Tel: (714)-893-7594

Not your average street bike

Hooker

Hooker Headers
1032 W. Brook Street
Ontario, Calif. 91762
Tel: (714)-983-5871

Filters

K & N Engineering Inc.
561 Iowa Avenue
Riverside, Calif. 92502
Tel: (714)-682-8813

Disk Brake Components

Hurst/Airheart Products Inc.
20235 Bahama Street,
Chatsworth, Calif. 91311
Tel: (213)-882-6600

Chain

Diamond Chain Co.
402 Kentucky Avenue,
Indianapolis, Ind. 46225
Tel: (317)-638-6431

Gas Tanks

Don Vesco Products Inc.
7565 North Avenue
Lemon Grove, Calif. 90245
Tel: (714)-465-8256

5 One of the gladiators

HE IS SHORTER THAN YOU MIGHT IMAGINE FROM A PHOTOGRAPH AND WALKS WITH A BANDY GAIT FROM TOO MANY YEARS SPENT ON A MOTORCYCLE. IN THE TOP OF HIS TOOL CHEST THERE ARE ALWAYS AT LEAST TWO PACKS OF CIGARETTES, ONE OF WHICH HE WILL REACH FOR WHEN HE TAKES OFF HIS HELMET. HE MAY NOT SEEM THE ATHLETIC TYPE, BUT PUT HIM ON ANY TYPE OF RACING MOTORCYCLE AND WATCH HIM GO. MEET ONE OF THE MOST CONTINUALLY SUCCESSFUL AND WELL-LIKED MOTORCYCLE RACERS IN THE USA. MEET GENE ROMERO.

Should you meet Gene anywhere other than a racetrack you would probably be hard pressed to guess his occupation, for though it is changing, there is an image the public has of motorcycle racers. While dirty fingernails, an old sweat-soaked grimy T-shirt, long greasy unkempt hair and something of a hell raiser might be the image, it is so far from the truth as to be ludicrous in the extreme. The man who meets you at the door of his expensive apartment is always neatly, though casually, dressed; his hair gives the impression of having been styled ten minutes before and he is always clean shaven. Once inside another surprise awaits. Even though he lives alone (some of the time anyway - this is no monk) the well furnished apartment is spotless, with the bed always made and no dirty dishes in the sink. But before you get the impression this is a mausoleum doubling as somewhere to live, there are chinks in the armor. The refrigerator is literally covered in decals of one sort or another and the rock music eminating from a huge stereo has to be turned down before anyone can be heard. I mention all this only to destroy whatever preconceived ideas some might have of professional racers, and to show that Gene Romero runs his life much as he does his racing career - business like, clean and everything in order - which in part are some of the reasons why he is successful where others are not.

Born nearly thirty years ago in the northern California town of Martinez, and later resident in San Louis Obispo, Gene had no intentions of becoming a motorcycle racer. Cars and especially race cars held his interest, so with encouragement from an enthusiastic father he began racing quarter midgets at the age of nine, turning to go-karts soon after.

If he hadn't needed some mode of transport on which to get to school, the young Romero might never have purchased a motorcycle; his introduction to the world of two wheels was a Triumph Tiger Cub. Too young to have a license, he stayed off the streets in the then much more rural area, and played at racing in a field across the street from his parents' house.

On a dare from his father, Gene entered an AMA amateur TT scramble at the age of fourteen - and won. With more wins under his belt, the Cub was soon replaced by a new 1963 model and then a 250cc Bultaco.

Enamored with his success, Gene (as he readily admits) was 'pretty good at shooting off at the mouth'. Yet much of what he boasted about was warranted. After all, with less than a

One of the gladiators

year's experience in riding a motorcycle, he had progressed from novice to junior to top 250cc expert in AMA district 35. With the minimum age for racing professionally then set at eighteen (as opposed to sixteen today) his claims of racing professionally and 'beating all those other guys' had a hollow ring at only fifteen years of age. His father, however, had other ideas. With the aid of a phony birth certificate, Gene Romero received a novice professional license from the AMA. It wasn't as though his father was pushing him, it was simply that after being associated with automobile racing for so many years, he recognized talent. And if Gene, biting his fingernails on his first trip down to Ascot Park, was less than confident, his father was not.

In those halcyon days of Ascot there were always far too many riders entered; this particular TT was no exception. With 130 novices entered, only the winners of each heat were assured of a place in the final. Gene won his heat, then went on to win the final.

Within two months of the birth of 1964's racing season as a novice, Gene had enough

Above left Single digit National numbers are assigned to former Grand National Champions; number 3 is Gene Romero's trademark *(Bob Jackson)*

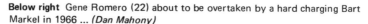

Below right Gene Romero (22) about to be overtaken by a hard charging Bart Markel in 1966 ... *(Dan Mahony)*

points accumulated to qualify for the next step up the ladder - the junior class. Unfortunately, the AMA rules don't permit or allow for this type of situation; consequently the TT ace from up the coast remained a novice for the rest of the year, but added to his victories the title of Number 1 Novice TT rider in the nation. Exactly the same situation prevailed the following year; the points to move onwards had been obtained by late April/early May, by which time the title upped one notch to the National Number 1 Junior TT rider. And if there was doubt in anyone's mind that Gene could not handle the flat tracks, they were to be disappointed. His progress was admittedly not as rapid, but he learnt from every outing, winning some and losing others.

When most other riders were beginning to race as novice professionals, Gene Romero was a first year expert, achieving a National number a year later at nineteen. Up until 1967 he raced during the summer months and worked in a motorcycle shop during the winter. The situation didn't really suit his employer for when needed, he was never there, and when there, he wasn't needed. The arrangement came to an abrupt halt. If up until then everything had been rolling along as if there were no tomorrows, 1967 was to be the turning point. Throughout his early career Gene had ridden his own TT bike and was sponsored in part on the flat tracks by Harley Davidson as a novice, and then by the US Triumph Distributors. With pockets still bulging from the previous season's wins he confidently started the 1967 season, but a badly broken leg was to keep him away from much of the season's racing. After weathering the hospital bills and a winter, the money and sponsorship had all disappeared.

1968 was to be the comeback year, but an early arrangement with Harley-Davidson failed to work out so Gene took to the road with his truck, one TT bike, two tires and his last $100 (£60). If a National TT win at Lincoln, Nebraska, plus places and wins in other races put Gene back on the road to liquidity, the year was also important in that it changed his attitude to racing. If it was to be his profession, it would have to be run on more businesslike lines, with a program worked out in advance of each season.

By no means the first to run his racing life as a business, Gene has probably honed the approach much finer than many of his opponents. He made sure his appearance was acceptable to everyone in and out of motorcycling, and all presentations for sponsorship were made in a businesslike fashion, along with any material deemed necessary to help his case. In an age when extremely long hair and jeans were acceptable, many prospective sponsors could only have been impressed by the well groomed young man carrying a briefcase, who stood before them asking for money.

Yet this was only part of what was and still is required. A meticulous man by nature, his motorcycles were taken down to the last nut and bolt, then rebuilt (regardless of cost) to become as powerful and reliable as possible. The reasoning was quite obvious. Anytime a motor-cycle failed him, his earnings were in jeopardy. To this day, no one can remember seeing Gene working on an engine in the pits between races other than to perform the usual between race maintenance.

Taking care of where to race plus the finances was another aspect looked at fairly compre-hensively. In 1969, there were fewer races on the National schedule, which permitted more racing on off-weekends and during the week. Before the season had started, Gene had planned where he would race on these off-weekends and how much he would be paid. Using a large map of the country, the distances and expenses and money involved were taken into account, before accepting. This was to ensure he was getting the best deal for his outlay, considering where he might have to be a week or a few days later, and how much it might cost to get there. The money side was run like any business, with profit and loss columns, with a reserve fund for weeks or months when he might be injured or fail to win any money.

In a country where advertising and selling yourself is all part of normal living, the nickname 'Burritto' (usually spelt with only one 't') from his Spanish heritage was adopted, to help every-one remember his name. Although he no longer lived there, his home town of San Luis Obispo was kept on file with the AMA in order to help further this end. After all, how many riders named 'Burritto' are there, much less from a town called San Luis Obispo?

If there is some doubt as to the effect of all these measures, Gene Romero was runner up

One of the gladiators

... and in 1976 on the Evel Knievel Harley-Davidson *(Bob Jackson)*

Above The year 1970, new Grand National Champion Romero (Triumph) poses with runner up Jim Rice (BSA) and third place finisher Dave Aldana (BSA) *(Dan Mahony)*

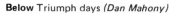

Below Triumph days *(Dan Mahony)*

One of the gladiators

to the National Champion in 1969, National Champion in 1970, has never placed lower than number 10 since, is one of the best known motorcycle racers in the world and has a healthy bank account.

Nothing ever stays the same forever though. There have been ups and downs for which any big time racer must be prepared. From being a full-time Yamaha factory rider in 1974, the sponsorship was reduced to just road race machinery in 1975, when Yamaha began to tighten the belt on its race program. At the end of the 1975 season, Gene was axed completely in a further cutback and though still a force to be reckoned with, he was again back to the ranks of riders seeking sponsorship. His only comments, 'It's just like any job; there is always the chance you will be laid off. I have to prepare for the possibility so I can weather out the lean times.'

Nearing the completion of the first lap of the main event at the September 1976 San Jose 25 mile National, Gene (center picture No.3) is about to pick off a bunch of riders down the straight *(Bob Jackson)*

Through the contacts and friends made over the years, the quest was not as tough as had been in the past. His friend, Evel Knievel, though not needing any exposure, was looking for some way to put back into motorcycling something of what he had taken out, consequently, an arrangement was reached whereby he sponsored two XR750's for the miles and half-miles. Don Vesco supplied a TZ750 Yamaha for the road races, Gene already had a 360cc Yamaha short tracker, and the trusty TT bike was again pressed into service.

With a racing career already spanning twenty years, Gene has travelled many miles to and from races. Anyone considering this nomadic life who assumes the travelling is all milk and honey should carefully consider Gene's 1976 season.

The bulk of the National schedule can be broken down into segments - the races in the East and Mid-west, and the races in the West. For Gene, the longest periods away from home in Los Angeles were from May 22 to July 5, and August 11 to September 20. During these two approximate seven week periods, he bases himself in Indianapolis, driving to wherever the racing might be. For some races, such as Terre Haute, very little driving and additional accommodation are required, but others such as Loudon, New Hampshire or Talledega, Alabama, require much more. Wednesday nights will find many of the professionals over in Hinsdale, Illinois, with Tuesday nights reserved for St. Louis. Both are popular weekly non-National short track events, ridden to keep in shape and for adding a few extra bucks to the kitty.

Arriving home on July 5 after racing in Albuquerque the previous day, preparations are made to drive to Northern California and Washington, a mile race at San Jose on July 10 and a TT at Castle Rock on the 17. It's back up to Monterey for a road race on August 1, back home and to Ascot Park for a TT on the 7. September 26, one week after returning home from the second swing back East, finds Gene again at San Jose, but then the last two races, a road race at Riverside and a half-mile at Ascot, are within spitting distance of his home.

Above Romero's adopted nickname of a Mexican culinary delight appears on his van license plate *(Author)*

Below Baby, you orta be in pictures! *(Bob Jackson)*

One of the gladiators

Should you already be breathless, this is only part of the miles travelled. There was an airplane trip to Norfolk, Virginia, for a short track race just prior to Christmas 1975, and another at New Year to Indianapolis for the same type of event. Mid-January required a road trip to Houston, Texas; early March saw everyone heading to Daytona. Early April there was again a race in Texas, this time Dallas, with the second of four San Jose races in mid-May. Interspersed between these early dates were races in San Diego, Phoenix, Northern California and one at Ascot. If this wasn't enough, there was also about a week spent in England for the annual Easter Anglo-American road races, another trip to Daytona for promotional purposes and one to AMA headquarters in Ohio for a professional rules committee meeting, of which Gene is a representative. Two more trips to Phoenix brought the total races for the year to between 50 and 60 and involved some 90,000 to 100,000 miles travelling.

For anyone undertaking such a demanding routine, the inevitable question 'Is it worth it?' always crops up. For Gene the answer is unequivocally 'Yes' for since 1970 (the year he became National Champion) he has never grossed less than $50,000 (£30,000) in prize and start money. The net or figure on which taxes and social security is paid is naturally lower because the expenses incurred in earning the money are legitimate business deductions, and only Gene plus the Internal Revenue Service are privy to the actual take-home earnings. For those wondering how taxes are paid by a man who doesn't really know how much he might make in a year, estimated earnings with the tax payable must be filed quarterly. Estimate on the light side and the government subjects the taxpayer to a penalty plus interest charges.

In the main, Gene's expenses are limited to paying for food and motels en route to and from the National Meetings. Although he maintains the two XR750 Harley-Davidson dirt trackers himself, the cost of their upkeep is born by his sponsor, as is that of the Yamaha road racer. Tires and lubricants are also taken care of by sponsoring rubber and oil companies.

For the majority of non-National events, Gene receives start (or appearance) money plus travelling and lodging expenses. The amount varies from promoter to promoter as there is no set scale. The promoter knows the crowd drawing appeal of individual riders and how much he is prepared to pay; the rider knows his own worth and how much he is prepared to accept. While $300 (£180) plus motel and gas money is a ball park figure, Gene has received as high as $1,000 (£600).

Up until and including 1976, Gene has campaigned every National race. Only now in 1977 is he considering slackening the pace by foregoing the TT's and short track events. He has wanted more time for developing some business ventures and an overwhelming desire to try USAC Indianapolis type race cars should also materialize this year. Before any mention of retirement is made, he quickly adds that 'There's still a lot of motorcycle racing left in the old dog yet.'

The reasons for including this chapter have been twofold. There are many enthusiasts who pay to watch professional racing and want to know more about the lives of the professionals, but have no way of doing so because the high fence between the racetrack and the grandstand is too effective a barrier in many ways. Yet this was not the prime purpose. Many younger riders with talent have no knowledge of what is involved in becoming, and more importantly staying, an employed professional racer. Talent will out; one way or another it always does, but as we have seen, talent to stay solvent and continue racing is also a requirement.

If the intention has been to show through the continuing career of one man that fame, and success are attainable goals, the life - though a good one - is also precarious. There has to be tenacity when the chips are down and a certain amount of restraint when the pockets are full. The good life comes to no one who isn't prepared to serve the necessary apprenticeship in these two areas. The way to the top is not easy as anyone there will testify. An 'overnight' success has usually spent many years perfecting his craft out of the limelight. Gene Romero is only now beginning to relax and enjoy the fruits of those long, though enjoyable, years. He sums it up very well with this simple piece of advice: 'Pay your dues and hang in there. Your turn will come.'

One of the gladiators

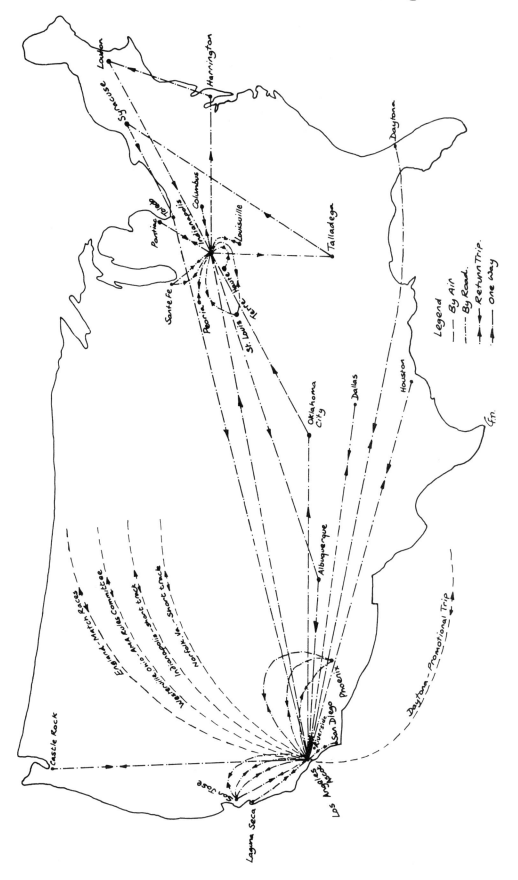

Figure 1. Gene Romero's 1976 racing season mileage (Author)

85

One of the gladiators

Wearing white leathers is Romero's answer to being seen and avoided by other riders should he fall
(Bob Jackson)

6 Keep on truckin'

PROFESSIONAL FLAT TRACKERS SPEND MANY HOURS IN THEIR
VEHICLES TRAVELLING TO AND FROM RACES: THE VEHICLES HAVE
BY NECESSITY TO BE BOTH RELIABLE AND COMFORTABLE. WHETHER
YOU ARE CONSIDERING THE NOMADIC LIFE OF THE PROFESSIONAL
RIDER, OR ARE SITTING ACROSS AN OCEAN WANTING TO KNOW MORE
ABOUT HOW AMERICAN MOTORCYCLE RACERS TRAVEL, THIS
CHAPTER IS OFFERED AS BOTH INFORMATIVE AND ENTERTAINING
READING.

The vastness of the continental United States is hard to comprehend unless you've
travelled across its three thousand miles by road. A jet plane can wisk you from New York to
California in a little over 5 hours, but the same journey by road will take 60 hours at legal
speeds. I well remember my first road trip around this continent, for although I knew pretty
well what to expect, I was still surprised by the contrasts I found. From forests in the east to
mountains and deserts in the west; huge plains in the mid-west growing mile upon mile of
grain, to alligator swamps in the south, made any new destination an adventure. A few years
have passed, but I always look forward to travel by road, for there are still countless places to
see, people to meet and forgotten experiences to re-live. Airplanes and railroads may play a big
part in the moving of people and freight, but the roads are the lifelines of any nation. And it is
down on the roads of America the riders, mechanics, wives, lovers and children who follow the
professional flat track circuit can be found lugging bikes, spares and equipment many thousands
of miles during a year.

The situation is very similar to the professional motocross or road race circuit in Europe;
riders zig-zag across the country during the summer months to races that occur almost every
week, as do the professionals in Europe who instead chase across countries. But here the
similarity ends, for in the United States the distances are far greater, demanding in many
instances the riders waiting around only long enough to pick up their winnings before leaving
to drive halfway across the country for the next race.

Driving in the US is still a way of life, for unlike people in other developed countries,
Americans continue their love affair with the automobile. The oil embargo of 1974 made
everyone aware the world's supply of oil was not infinite, and to some extent changes have
affected driving and driving habits in this country. The price of petroleum doubled and a
supposedly gas saving 55 mph speed limit was introduced nationwide. For a while smaller
imported vehicles did command a sizeable chunk of sales, but no one foresaw the continuing
love the American people have for their large, gas-guzzling monsters, the sales of which
continue almost unabated.

The term 'gas-guzzling Detroit barge' is really an enigma, for it is surprising how many
miles these monsters will go on a gallon of gasoline. A reasonably loaded van with a 318 cubic
inch (5.25 liters) V8 engine, equipped with power steering and automatic transmission, will

Keep on truckin'

Forceful riding by Dave Aldana *(Dan Mahony)*

average about 14 miles per gallon (16.8 miles per Imperial gallon) at 55 miles per hour on the highway; considerably more than one would first imagine for a vehicle in the four to five thousand pound weight class.

It seems all motorcycle racers, whether amateur or professional, hate to work on their vehicles and only do so out of necessity. All will work diligently into the wee small hours rebuilding a blown engine, whereas even changing the plugs in the truck becomes a major operation put off until the vehicle either stops, runs atrociously, or won't start. Travelling backwards and forwards across the country requires a reliable vehicle, and if nothing else, V8 engines are incredibly reliable, requiring only a minimum of maintenance. By now you may have realized I am completely sold on American automobile engineering. The vehicles I have owned have given the reliability I crave during my trips around the country, except for one which it may be worthwhile mentioning. Large displacement engines have a definite advantage over their smaller brothers; they can be terribly sick with a serious ailment but when a 200 horse engine loses 50 horsepower it can still continue on as I am about to relate.

While driving a pickup truck loaded down with two bikes and lots of tools across country, one cylinder stopped firing just as 27,000 miles rolled over on the odometer - 27,000 for the second time that is. The cylinder had been sucking oil for some time and a cracked piston was suspected, but we carried on to our destination in Pennsylvania on seven cylinders, a distance of some six hundred miles, with only a minimum loss of power noticeable, mainly on steep upgrades. With the head removed the diagnosis proved correct. No time was available to rebuild the engine so a trip was made to the local car dismantler where a substitute 327 cubic inch (5.36 liters) engine from a wrecked car was purchased for $75 (£50). The engine was installed within two days and we were on our way again. Where else in the world in 1975 was it possible to buy a huge used engine for such a low figure and still have it giving good service 30,000 miles later? American made engines are heavy and overbuilt, but I know of no other production gasoline engine capable of regularly going over 100,000 miles without even a top end overhaul.

The most favored vehicles for transporting bikes around the country are, in order of preference: vans, campers and motorhomes. Vans head up the list for a variety of reasons, but campers and motorhomes are not uncommon transport. It would be hard to generalize who uses what, but suffice to say only a very few riders have a $25,000 (£15,000) motorhome at their disposal.

The omnipresent Dodge van which comes in various styles and lengths is a favorite of motorcycle racers *(Author)*

In the last few years the lowly van has become extremely popular, not only with motorcyclists, but practically every segment of the population, and various models are available from either General Motors, Ford or Chrysler. Most are sold with an automatic transmission, power steering, power brakes and air conditioning. Those unfamiliar with summers in this country might assume the air conditioning to be superfluous, but the heat and humidity of the Eastern and Midwestern states can leave one drained of energy and drenched in sweat even when just sitting behind the steering wheel. Power steering and power brakes are almost mandatory as trying to steer or stop these monsters would sap the strength of a Samson in a very short while.

With many riders deciding on a van for their jaunts across country, I will list some modifications or additions usually carried out on this popular vehicle. The modifications fall into two categories: those necessary to improve the comfort or handling and those purely cosmetic, to improve the looks.

Keep on truckin'

The list of cosmetic modifications available are numerous with the only limiting factor being the thickness of an owner's wallet. One cosmetic accessory which has become almost mandatory is a 'trick' set of wide wheels and tires, to replace the standard set which came with the vehicle. The argument of getting more rubber to the road to improve handling in this case is irrelevant, as the majority of roads in this country do not wind as they do in Europe. The shortest distance between two points is a straight line and most highways are built on this principle. However 'trick' wheels, either aluminum or the latest fabricated steel-spoked type, do improve the looks of most vans and low profile square sided tires or fat radials make an otherwise ordinary van look something special — even if it isn't.

Not completely necessary, but highly recommended because of varying loads a van may have to carry (extra bikes maybe), is a set of adjustable air shock absorbers to replace the standard units at the rear of the van. When the load is excessive and the headlights blind everyone, even when dipped, a quick trip into a gas station to pump up the shocks with an air hose is all that is necessary to bring the body back to its original level position. Should the weight be far more than the van can carry, and is lugged around constantly, a stronger set of springs would be advisable to complement the air shocks. There are many long and lonely stretches of road in the US where it is prudent not to be stopped with a broken spring.

Most of us are basically lazy and a pleasant addition to the air shock conversion is the electrically-operated compressor, located under the hood. The compressor is connected by air hoses to the rear shocks and is activated by a switch on the instrument panel. A pressure gauge shows the pressure in the shocks.

On vehicles with air shocks the height of the rear end can be adjusted from the driver's seat to compensate for the load *(Author)*

90

Keep on truckin'

One other modification guaranteed to create a friendly atmosphere in any gas station is the addition of long range fuel tanks which supplement the standard gas tank, and are usually hidden from the attendant's view beneath the chassis. Properly valved and connected there is no work involved changing over from empty to full tanks and the existing filler will also fill the auxillary tanks. Any vehicle containing motorcycles automatically prompts a conversation, but when the gas pump continues delivering after twenty gallons have not quenched the monster's thirst, a crowd usually gathers demanding to know where it is all going.

Tanks are available which fit very conveniently inside the van as well as underneath, taking up very little space which could be used for anything else, and a total capacity of around 60 or more US gallons has its advantages. If you normally stop to fill up every 250 miles, your range has been effectively increased three times, something worth considering if driving all night. For although we seem to be a twenty four hour non-stop society, there are parts of the country in which gas stations close soon after sunset. The nagging feeling in the back of one's mind that the vehicle will run out of gas miles from anywhere during the night is all but eliminated with auxiliary tanks.

If just one reason for increased gas capacity had to be cited, then saving money would be it. During these times of high fuel prices it is still refreshing to find areas in which prices have not increased to as much as you may now be experiencing, consequently a ten cent a gallon saving soon adds up when purchasing 60 gallons at a time.

One word of warning. Insurance companies tend to frown on auxiliary fuel tanks, possibly because some have been badly installed and fires developed in accidents. If you are considering this type of conversion, check with your insurance company first.

The battery is one accessory usually neglected, but much progress has been made recently in producing batteries which require little or no maintenance. One type which has been available from J.C. Penney auto departments, and is now standard equipment on some new cars, is the completely sealed battery. Needing no water, periodic checking or cleaning, the hood can be closed and the battery forgotten. Gone also is the two year guarantee, after which the battery seemingly expires at 12:01am into the third year. Many batteries are now guaranteed for as long as the buyer owns the vehicle.

It should not be forgotten the prime objective is to transport racing motorcycles and some type of securing method is necessary to keep them from moving around. Quick release tie down straps, the most widely used method, are inexpensive and can be relied upon. Eye bolts secured through the floor provide the necessary anchor points at one end, while the handlebars serve adequately at the other. With the tie downs loose, hooked through the eye bolts and over the 'bars, preferably at a bend close to the steering head, the straps are then pulled tight until the front suspension is squashed down. The force of the fork springs trying to return to their original position against the pull of the straps is more than sufficient restraint to keep the bike from moving.

Though expensive, seats may be worth replacing should the originals have sagged or offer none of the lower back support so necessary for enduring many hours at the wheel. One of the favorites now available is a high-backed type with arm and headrests, known as a Captain's Chair. Extremely comfortable and adjustable in all directions, the seat also swivels, a definite advantage should you decide to have a few friends over for a beer after a race. At least the host can have a decent chair, if everyone else has to sit on the wheelwells or floor.

In the last few years a new breed of businesses have emerged which cater to the egos of the ever increasing number of van owners. It is possible (again, money forthcoming) to have the complete interior decorated as one would a bedroom or living room, with beds, couches, carpet covered walls and even concealed lighting. Should this extension of personality appeal to you, remember, however careful a certain amount of oil and grease always manages to find its way into a racer's transport. And while there are exotic creations carrying around motor-cycles, the majority reserve the cargo part of the van for its intended purpose.

Although decorating the interior may not be to your taste, some work may be required should sleeping in your van become necessary. As anyone who has slept in a van can testify, the right weather conditions produce condensation and the interior walls and roof stream

Keep on truckin'

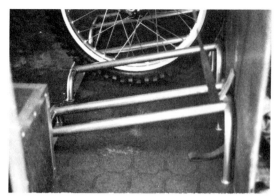

Preset tiedowns and some fixed arrangement to hold the front wheel is a must if the machine is to remain upright while in transit *(Author)*

with water. This can become uncomfortable during the night, even more so in the morning when finding one's clothes are soaking wet and someone borrowed your last clean T-shirt the day before. Lining the inside, if it isn't already done, with panelling while begging, stealing, or in the last resort buying plywood to cover the floor (it also soaks up the oil) is generally a good solution.

Although many professionals install a bunk above the seats, this is usually used only when travelling across country to a race. There is an inherent trait in all racers to get in a vehicle and drive nonstop for 2,000 miles to a race, although this is only achieved when two people can share the driving and if time is limited. A more leisurely pace permits overnight stops in motels and in the towns in which the various races are held.

Should you not live in, or have not visited the United States, it may be worth digressing for a moment to explain the attitudes and habits of Americans regarding eating and sleeping when on the road. There is a tremendous abundance of good eating and sleeping places across the country, all vying for the customer's dollar. Indeed, the competition between all of them keeps the standards high and the prices down.

The motel business is very large and it seems every town across the country has its motel row, with rooms ranging in price from expensive, $20 (£12) a night for a single (no food included) down to $6 (£3.50). The higher priced motel is usually loaded with luxuries such as vibrating beds, which soothe away the bad aches of a day's drive! The $6 versions are clean with good beds, a shower and maybe a television, but here the luxury stops; they are ideal places to sleep and the price is well within the reach of most travellers.

Fast food restaurants are appearing around the world, in vast numbers, and most are American owned. The revolving bucket thirty feet up in the air, on which is the face of a Kentucky Colonel, is one of the better known, and while I do not advocate eating chicken every night, it is a credit to the franchise food industry that wherever one goes the quality is usually pretty good.

There are many of these types of restaurants to be found around the country, serving everything from hamburgers to roast beef. They are easily spotted, for a Kentucky Fried Chicken place is as easily identifiable by its appearance in Phoenix, Arizona, as it is in Jacksonville, Florida. When travelling on a limited budget it is easy to be sucked into a strange restaurant, only to find the food not up to scratch and the prices out of sight. But the prices and menus at fast food restaurants are almost without exception the same across the country.

And although eating at these places may become boring after a while, one knows what to expect as regards quantity and quality. With everything so convenient and reasonably priced, it isn't hard to see why the majority, including racers, take advantage of the services at their disposal rather than camping, fitting out their vans, or buying campers or motorhomes. It really isn't necessary to lay out a large amount of money on exotic creature comforts when they are so readily available, and besides, who wants to sleep in a van when a good bed and shower are available.

Having said all that, it would seem there is no case for owning a camper or motorhome, but nothing could be further from the truth, for this is a country of different strokes for different folks. In the majority of cases the racer's transport is geared, like the rest of us, to how much he can afford. Vans fit the bill for a variety of reasons and are a reasonably attainable goal. A camper or motorhome makes for being completely independent in a rest area off a highway, or at a race becomes a home away from home, but fully equipped, these are expensive investments, the cost of which has to be weighed against the use. For instance, can the price be justified when it stands idly in the driveway throughout the winter? Or what resale value can be expected when the time comes to sell? The fact that two people can eat in restaurants and sleep in motels for several race seasons and probably never spend more than half the initial cost of a motorhome is possibly never taken into consideration. Yet many people like this form of transport, and as I am trying to cover all aspects of transporting motorcycles, it would be unfair to leave them out.

A camper may be known by a different name in other countries, but to an American, it is a mobile home which rests in the carrying box of a pick-up truck. They are unique in that should the camper not be needed, it can be quickly taken out to be left standing in the driveway. The procedure is relatively simple. A few retainers are loosened, the four legs extended to the ground, and then slightly jacked up to allow the pick-up truck to be driven away. The reverse procedure puts the camper back into the pick-up at the weekends or whenever needed.

Most campers come equipped with beds, kitchen and toilet, but many other extras such as air conditioning and heat are available. Most follow the same design of locating a double bed over the cab while extra elbow room is obtained by making the camper slightly wider than the truck. The inside, like any camping vehicle the world over, is a good example of how much can

Many riders install a bunk up and behind the front seats of their vans for either the driver or passenger to sleep upon during non-stop cross-country runs *(Author)*

Keep on truckin'

A full size pick up with its slide in camper *(Author)*

GMC's entry into the motorhome market is this futuristic looking model *(Author)*

be built into such a limited space.

They also come in many sizes, although the larger they become, the more prone they are to being blown around by crosswinds. Across the deserts of the southwest winds blow extremely hard, and driving a large camper across hundreds of miles of open desert can be an experience in itself. Owners agree an adjustment in driving is necessary but most suggest parking the rig in high winds.

One problem with a camper is the limited floor space. The width of the floor is limited to the width of bed of the pick-up and while this poses no problem in normal use, there are problems when carrying a motorcycle. Most campers have a narrow entry door (this increases the amount of space available inside for cupboards, toilet, etc.) and the handlebars of any bike have to be removed to gain entry. This is not too much of a problem unless it has to be done often, but once inside the bike has to be secured and this severely limits the amount of space needed to move around in, or maybe prepare a meal. In most instances the bike has to be removed and replaced should the camper be used. One of the more obvious solutions is to pull a trailer which contains just the bikes and equipment, leaving the camper to be used as it was intended. However, this adds considerable weight to an already heavy vehicle and as extra weight means less miles per gallon, the extra addition of a trailer can have you pulling into gas stations more often than you can afford.

Before toting around a large camper, some work on the suspension usually in the form of helper springs and extra heavy duty shocks is considered an absolute necessity for coping with the additional weight.

Now consider a motorhome, the creme de la creme. There is no ambiguity here for the word describes the vehicle perfectly. This is the nearest thing to a home away from home. Only a manufacturer's brochure can really describe the splendour of some of these homes on wheels, but don't bank on getting one until you're Number 1 in motorcycle racing or have the winning ticket in the Irish Sweepstakes. Built on a specially prepared chassis from Detroit, the larger versions usually sleep up to six persons and can handle everyone inside at the same time, milling around while a meal is being prepared.

Gas consumption is usually high but if you are in this league such a mundane thing doesn't really matter. Creature comforts are well catered for and while on the road, it is not unusual to see a TV antenna bending against the wind atop the vehicle, while someone visible through the large windows is watching television. The floor space of a motorhome is considerably more spacious than a camper and will accommodate a motorcycle (or two) but then, a trailer is the only way to go for who wants a motorcycle in the living room!

Pick-up trucks were mentioned only briefly with regard to toting around campers, as by themselves they are not considered a suitable vehicle for hauling racing motorcycles around the

Although a new generation of longer, wider and more luxurious vans have edged out the pick up as racing transport, no look at American automobiles would be complete without a photograph of the popular El Camino car pick up *(Author)*

country. It is worth mentioning the reasons and styles available, for it also gives me the oportunity to write about my favorite vehicle, the car pick-up. I know of no European motorcycle racer who hasn't been fascinated at the first sight of either a Chevrolet El Camino or Ford Ranchero.

Racers everywhere are familiar with the problems of pick-up trucks, probably the ease with which any equipment can be stolen being the first which comes to mind. In this country, there is a large market for stolen motorcycles, parts, tools or accessories, and pick-ups are fair (or unfair, whichever side of the fence you happen to be on) game in parking lots of restaurants, motels, or anywhere left unattended. There is no really effective solution to the problem except putting everything readily moveable into the cab, but this becomes a hassle and is only a deterrent to amateurs. Precautions such as sitting at window booths in restaurants with the truck in full view helps, and parking in a well lighted spot in any motel lot goes a long way in ensuring a good night's sleep.

Neither is a tarpaulin the complete answer for although it keeps prying eyes and rain out, I have never seen a cover the wind didn't eventually get under and try to blow away. Keeping the thing folded and ready for use is probably the best idea, then in the emergency of a

Keep on truckin'

sudden summer thunderstorm, the machine can be protected from the deluge.

One of the two styles of pick-ups available is the high off the ground boxy shaped truck, workhorse of farmers and businesses. This is considered a standard sized truck and is the pattern around which most campers are built. The large volume of carrying capacity is ideal for motorcycles and equipment, but these trucks are extremely well built and heavy, which usually results in unacceptable gas mileage.

The other type available is, of course, the car pick-up, a favorite of motorcycle racers, but a truck which tends to be used more locally than for cross-country trips. The main disadvantage is the relatively small carrying space, yet this tends to be offset by its comfort and appearance. The cab has all the comforts of a car, indeed it is a car from the front bumper to where the carrying compartment begins, and even the bodywork around the pick-up bed is styled to be in keeping with the front of the vehicle. With a smaller frontal area than a van, it is considerably more miserly with a gallon of gasoline, while the car type suspension smoothes out the roughest of roads to make a long trip less tiring.

As an 'alien' who has adopted the US as home, I would like to direct a few words to those who can only gauge American automobile engineering from a distance. I well remember my own impressions, for in England the only source of information about American cars was the glossy advertisements which appeared in *Playboy* magazine and a couple of bad car magazines. With only pictures to look at, it was not possible to appreciate anymore than what was shown, and to most of us, the late 50s era of Jukebox styling — huge fins at the rear extending to the skies — didn't quite make it. Times changed and so did the styling, but early impressions tend to stick, especially when no first-hand experience is available to change an opinion. Only by spending time in the US is it possible to understand that the automobile is tailored to suit the country and needs of its people, for Americans practically live in their cars.

The majority require a soft, comfortable ride and this is best obtained with a long wheelbase and wide stance. Large V8 engines, which rarely turn over at more than 4000rpm, keep noise and vibration to a minimum, an important consideration if one is not to feel like a disaster area after 700 miles. Couple these features with cheap fuel and it is easy to see how and why the American car has evolved into a giant.

In time, the American car may become as extinct as the dodo bird, for already problems with diminishing supplies of raw materials and oil have signalled reductions in size and weight. But whatever the outcome this monster will be long revered by many of us who consider it the only way to fly.

CITIZEN BAND RADIOS

'Breaker, breaker, on channel one nine.'
'Go ahead breaker.'
'Yeah, this is Flyboy. Can someone give me a smokey report for my twenty. I'm heading east on highway 40 just passing exit 27. I'm a little late and want to put the hammer down but I don't want to pay out no green stamps for an invitation. C'mon.'
'That's a big 10-4 Flyboy. There's a smokey in a plain brown wrapper taking pictures from behind a bridge about four miles ahead of ya.'
'Thanks big buddy, we'll keep our eyes open.'

Amusing one's self, or cutting down on the boredom of a long drive was for years limited to listening to the radio, then along came eight track and cassette tape players. These items are now sold world wide but in the United States a citizen's band radio (or CB for short) is one item no self-respecting motorcycle racer would be without in his vehicle.

Citizen's band is 'ham' radio for the masses and sales are booming as the concept has caught the imagination of millions across the country. Many years ago the government allotted 23 (now 17 more as of January, 1977) radio frequencies on which anyone could operate either for business or pleasure. No test is required as voice communication is used, but certain requirements such as a license and using call letters are placed on users.

Keep on truckin'

A typical citizen's band radio with its hand held microphone *(Author)*

The radios, which include transmitter and receiver in one small package, usually no larger than an eight track tape player, went almost unnoticed until independent truckers around the country used them to organize blockades of highways during the Arab oil embargo of 1973-74 as a protest against oil shortages and high prices. The trucker's strikes brought them national attention, but when it was learned they had used two way radios from inside the trucks to organize the protests and that they were readily available to all, the sales literally took off overnight and haven't stopped since.

The units are easy to install, simple to use, and relatively inexpensive. For $40 to $200 (£25 to £120) plus the price of an antenna $10 to $50 (£6 to £30), and not forgetting a license, for which the fee has temporarily been suspended, anyone can join the airwaves. With the continuation of our (dare I say ridiculous) 55mph speed limit, a CB radio has almost become a necessity to keep abreast of police movements and radar speed traps along the highways, for almost no one is prepared to travel along wide open stretches of road at 55mph. Talking with passing trucks or cars can help wile away the hours at the wheel, and CB radio does have a serious application in that help can be summoned in the advent of an accident or breakdown.

The truckers developed their own language for use over the airways on which everyone is now hooked, and even replaced (much to government annoyance) the required identifying call letters at the beginning of a broadcast with 'handles', such as 'Dipstick', 'Pink Panther', 'Rubber Duck', etc.

Generally a week or so is required after installing a radio to pick up on and understand many of the conversations, let alone transmit one. However constant monitoring soon increases one's vocabulary and in no time at all anyone can become an expert CBer.

To end this chapter, a glossary of some better known CB slang is included, which in turn may help you, as a beginner, to understand better the language of the road. Should you live elsewhere than the United States the words and phrases will be of only passing interest if no air waves have been set aside for public use; however they are original, and sometimes funny, pieces of Americana which you may derive pleasure from reading.

GLOSSARY OF CB SLANG

Advertising — Police car with its lights on
Back door — Rear vehicle of two or more using CB and running together

Keep on truckin'

Beat the bushes — Lead vehicle of a group watching for speed traps

Bear — A police officer (See also Smokey)

Bear in the air — Police helicopter or plane used for traffic surveillance

Bear den — Police station

Bean store — Restaurant

Big 10-4 — Basically means 'OK message received' but more 'I am in agreement'

Breaker — 'This station would like to use this channel ' Usually given with channel number: 'Breaker, one nine '

Brown bottles — Beer

Brush your teeth and comb your hair — Police radar ahead

Camera — Radar

Catch you on the flip flop — Catch you on the radio on the return trip

Check the seat covers — Watch out for a female driver with her skirt pulled up

Clean — No police around

C'mon — 'It's your turn to transmit now' used in place of over

Cowboy Cadillac — An El Camino or Ford Ranchero

Cut some Z's — Get some sleep

Ears — CB radio, as in 'Have you got your ears on'

Eatum up — Restaurant

Eighteen wheeler — Any tractor-trailer rig

Evel Knievel — Motorcyclist

Fat load — Overweight load

Feed the bears — Pay a traffic ticket

Fluff stuff — Snow

Four wheeler — Car

Front door — Lead vehicle of two or more running together using CB

Good numbers -- As in 'All the good numbers to you' Regards and good wishes. See Threes and eights

Green stamps — Money

Ground clouds — Fog

Haircut palace — Low clearance bridge

Handle — Name chosen for use on CB radio

Harvey Wallbanger — Reckless driver

Hanging onto your mudflaps — Driving right behind you

Hole in the wall — Tunnel

Home 20 — Home town

Invitations Traffic tickets

Keep the shiny side up and the dirty side down — Don't have an accident

Keep your nose between the ditches and smokey out of your britches — Drive carefully and watch out for smokey

Loose boardwalk — Bumpy road

Mixmaster — Cloverleaf intersection

Monfort lane — Passing lane

Nap trap — Motel, hotel or rest area

Negatory — Negative

On the side — Standing by and listening

Portable parking lot Car transporter

Pickum up — Pickup truck

Plain wrapper — Unmarked police car. Usually given as 'Smokey in a plain brown wrapper'

Pregnant roller skate — Volkswagen Beetle

Pull the big switch — Turn off the CB radio

Put the hammer down — Go faster than the speed limit

Ratchet jaw — Talkative CBer

Rig — CB radio, also tractor trailer

Rocking chair — Vehicle between the front door and the back door

Roger Ramjet — Driver of a car going well in excess of the speed limit

Rollerskate — Compact or import car

Rolling road block — Car going under the speed limit and holding up traffic

Sailboat fuel — Running empty

Seatcovers — Passengers

Shake the trees and rattle the leaves — Front vehicle watch ahead, last vehicle watch behind

Skating rink — Slippery road

Smokey or Smokey the bear — Police officer

Smokey's got ears — Police with CB radio

Super skate — Sports car or high performance sedan

Super slab Major highway

Taking pictures — Using radar

Threes and eights — Best regards

Tijuana taxi — Identifiable police car

Train station — Traffic court that fines everyone

Truck 'em easy — Have a good trip

Twisted pair — Telephone

Twenty — Location (10-20)

Wall to wall bears — Heavy police patrol

Wall to wall and treetop tall — Receiving you loud and clear

Willy weaver — Drunk driver

Window washer — Rainstorm

X-ray machine — Radar

XYL — Wife (literally means ex-young lady)

Keep on truckin'

Chuck Palmgren *(Bob Jackson)*

7 The 1975 Grand National season

AT INDIANAPOLIS LATE IN THE SEASON, KENNY ROBERTS SHOWED UP WITH A MACHINE HE HOPED COULD SALVAGE HIS CHANCES OF A THIRD CONSECUTIVE NATIONAL TITLE. THE MACHINE — A TZ750 YAMAHA FOUR CYLINDER, TWO-STROKE ROAD RACE ENGINE IN A DIRT TRACK FRAME — WAS PROBABLY THE MOST POWERFUL, EXOTIC AND AWE-INSPIRING MOUNT EVER TO BE SEEN AT A FLAT TRACK RACE.

When the Yamaha TZ700 mass produced road race bike was initially shown to the public in 1973, (it was later increased in size to 750cc and designated TZ750) many expressed concern for any rider who would attempt to ride one, while others were more concerned about the direction in which American pavement racing was going. The original concept behind road racing was basically the same as dirt track: good competitive racing on near identical machines which anyone could buy. Over the years, the rules have been modified, the net result being machines costing more and more money, going faster and faster and consequently hardly ever a privateer at the front of the pack. The TZ seemed to be just another nail in the coffin, but at least now the privateer on one of the Japanese machines would be a force to be reckoned with. The doubters case was much weaker and time has proved them wrong. The fact is that motorcycle racers are much more intelligent than many would give them credit for, and all immediately developed a respect for a machine which, if not given 100% concentration, could inflict a vast amount of damage to a body cast off at the high speeds of which it was capable.

The rest is history. Riders on TZ750s have won virtually every US major road race without any serious accidents occurring, but it must be said many of them are concerned with the ever-increasing speeds. Eyeballs literally jump up and down in their sockets with the vibration at 180mph and uneven track surfaces, and braking markers become blurs at the end of straightaways.

Motorcycle racers being what they are, it was only a matter of time before someone gave thought to building a miler around a TZ engine. The honor appears to go to Steve Baker, a road racer and flat tracker, who got together with Doug Schwerma of the now defunct Schwerma Products Company, makers of Champion frames. Shoehorning exotic engines into frames was not alien to Schwerma, for he had built frames for Kawasaki 3 cylinder triples and even a Honda four. The Kawasaki in the hands of Scott Brelsford became the first two-stroke ever to win an AMA expert event and although these machines put out lots of horsepower, they never achieved the notoriety the TZ did. With the only upcoming mile later in the season at Indianapolis some 2,000 miles away, there was no place to try out the finished machine other than Ascot Park, California, on a half-mile track with Rick Hocking aboard. Hocking proved the bike was competitive and five other frames were built.

One went to Kenny Roberts, who now enters the picture. For Roberts, 1975 hadn't been a good year. He was trying for his third consecutive title but had been dogged by minor

The 1975 Grand National season

The incredible TZ750 flat tracker *(Yamaha Motor Corp and Cycle World)*

mechanical problems and a violent crash at Castle Rock, Washington. Things had started off fairly smoothly with a TT win in the Houston Astrodome, and he was expected to carry off the Daytona 200 mile road race but his Yamaha's clutch had given out while in the lead. After bouncing back with a win at the Dallas short track, which put him at the head of the title chase, he then ran fifth at San Jose, thirteenth at Louisville, and fourth at Harrington, Delaware, before things really started to turn sour. A broken condenser wire kept him out of the final at Columbus, next came the crash at Castle Rock, followed by transmission trouble at Ascot when leading a TT. The problems seemed to go on forever, and the man who was out-distancing him was factory Harley-Davidson racer, Gary Scott, runner up in the title for the past three years, whom Roberts had been racing against since both were 16 year old novices at Ascot Park. Having won two Nationals and racked up points by placing well in the majority of the others, Scott held a comfortable lead by late August. For all his bad luck, Roberts was still second, although he knew the 750cc Yamaha four-stroke twin was no match for the ultra-rapid Harleys on mile courses. With three mile races remaining he needed all the points he could get. The factory, and indeed many private Harleys, had been enjoying phenomenal success on the dirt tracks in 1975, with the horsepower really showing on the long tracks. So swift were they down the straights the Yamaha riders were unable to catch the slipstream which could have helped make up for the difference in horsepower.

Thus the stage was set for what many have described as the most fantastic mile race ever - Indianapolis 1975.

No less than five riders arrived at Indianapolis with Schwerma framed TZ750s: Ken Roberts, Randy Cleek, Rick Hocking, Steve Baker and Skip Aksland. Don Vesco, with the remaining frame, was totally involved with becoming the fastest man in the world on two wheels and hadn't gotten around to building the machine for anyone.

All five riders pitted together and immediately a large crowd gathered. As many were seeing the bikes for the first time, their amazement was apparent. After all, here were the riders and mechanics going about their preparations on virtually untried one hundred horse-power machines as though it were an everyday occurrence.

A few changes had been made to the first machine after Hocking's initial ride, not the least of which were the stiffening gussets added to the drive side of the frame, and the need

Roberts about as far sideways as he ever wanted to get with the four cylinder rocket *(Dan Mahony)*

for a stronger rear axle and hub. The problem with the hub stemmed from the lack of distance between the bearings which, although more than adequate for the horsepower of any twin, could not cope with the power surges of the four. A completely new hub was machined from a solid billet with provision for four bearings (two on each side), spaced as wide as the swing arm would allow.

But even so, the TZs were not without their race day problems. Gearing didn't work out as pre-planned during practise, yet this was expected as the bikes had never run on anything except a half mile track. Hocking's bike seized one cylinder, Cleek's never ran right all day due to some mysterious electrical ailment, and Baker, with too much road racing under his belt, was having trouble getting back into the swing of things. Aksland got around fairly respectably, and so did Roberts.

Roberts put himself into the National final by qualifying and winning one of the two semi-final races. In the final, he used his tremendous horsepower and acceleration advantage on the straights to come from behind and finally blast his way past the surprised leading duo of Corky Keener and Jay Springsteen, who didn't see him coming until it was too late.

The TZ was the first two-stroke ever to win a National but it hadn't been easy, and tremendous credit must go to Roberts for bringing off what many thought was the impossible. After all, the machine came into the race virtually untried and definitely an unknown quantity, and the annals of motorcycling are littered with the memories of machines which were going to change racing but never got out of the starting gate. To the spectators, the sight of Roberts trying to control the 100mph slides while the TZ spewed up rooster tails of dirt, would long be remembered, although many could see the machine was difficult to ride and had problems putting its immense power to the ground. And, while no conclusions could be drawn, the concensus of opinion was that Kenny had put himself back into contention for the title as there was no way Harley-Davidson could come up with great gobs of horsepower before the next mile race at Syracuse in New York state. Everything wasn't roses though as Roberts didn't like the bike, saying quite openly after the race, 'They don't pay me enough to ride the thing.' The remark was widely publicized and unbeknown to everyone, the death knell had begun to sound for the four cylinder rocket from Japan.

The 1975 Grand National season

Roberts being chased by Steve Morehead at San Jose *(Dan Mahony)*

And so, on to Syracuse.

Unfortunately, the only thing Syracuse proved was that the TZ couldn't be ridden on every mile track. It was so hard and slippery that the power went up in wheelspin and Roberts chose to ride his four-stroke twin on which he lapped two seconds faster. Scott, meantime, had a definite psychological advantage over Roberts. The Yamaha twin was not competitive and both he and Roberts knew it. Yet, the advantage was not completely one sided as race director Dick O'Brien did not instruct the other Harley-Davidson teamsters to hang back and let Scott go if he got to the front. The factory bikes are as near identical as can be, everyone is treated equally, the rider must make the difference being the policy. Whether right or wrong, O'Brien, like many others in flat track racing, tries determinedly to hang onto this concept. Many must have thought him a man with a heart of stone, yet he has to be admired for standing by his principles, and no doubt, deep down his stomach was as knotted as Scott's.

Scott got on to the first row in the final by finishing second in his heat race, then it was Robert's turn. Working through the field after a lousy start, he crashed hard into the hay bales while going around the outside of a slower rider, who got completely sideways and out of control. Nothing was broken, but badly bruised and shaken Roberts had to call it a day with not one point added to his total. The same accident could just as easily have put Gary Scott out for the day, and while no one worth his salt enjoys winning under such circumstances, the opportunity for widening the points gap to almost impossible proportions was suddenly a reality — providing he did well in the final. The Gods, however, were not on Scott's side either that particular day. His usually reliable Harley had gearbox problems and he limped home in the 7th place, collecting only 44 points.

Roberts was still hanging in there as they moved on to Ohio.

There was no question of the TZ being brought out at Toledo because the Yamaha four-stroke twin was reasonably competitive on half-mile tracks. The shorter straights did not give the Harley riders the opportunity of pulling away as they could on the 130mph mile courses, and things in general looked brighter for Roberts. But again a bad start in the final left him in the middle of the pack. At the flag, Scott was second while Roberts finished in sixth place.

Now the writing was really on the wall. The points differential (338) was enough of a

104 cushion for Scott to take the Championship at the next race, providing he finished ahead of

The 1975 Grand National season

All TZ750 mounted at San Jose during practice; Kenny Roberts (1), Rick Hocking (13), Randy Cleek (29), and Skip Akslund *(Dan Mahony)*

Roberts. In what position Scott finished was of no consequence, just so long as Roberts was behind him.

The next race, the following week September 21, at San Jose, California, on the other side of the country — a mile track: Robert's sole chance of staying in contention — the incredible TZ750. If he could only bring off another Indianapolis, he could clinch the title with wins on Ascot Park's half-mile (September 27) and Ontario's road race course (October 5). All big ifs, but Roberts knew if it came down to the wire at Ontario, the edge would be with him.

After the Syracuse race, changes had been made to the TZ to try and correct some of the problems of putting the one hundred horsepower plus to the ground. The engine had been made to sit lower and further forward in the frame, while road race wheels and tires were fitted, which in turn lowered the complete machine. The gearbox of Scott's bike had been lovingly rebuilt so now all was ready for another great battle.

The California sun didn't come out on the 21st, but this was an advantage for the two-stroke men. Water and calcium had been added to the track during the week and as long as the over-cast held, the surface might just stay moist enough for the two-strokes to work, whereas any strong sun would dry out the course and make for a repeat performance of Syracuse.

Although only four of the TZs were entered: Roberts, Cleek, Hocking and Aksland, the two-stroke ranks were swelled with the two previously made Schwerma-framed Kawasaki 750cc triples of Scott Brelsford and Don Castro. These machines had run at Indianapolis (and like the Yamahas were parked at Syracuse), but their performance had been overshadowed by Roberts' incredible win. With more development, almost a year, and definitely more tractable than the TZs, the Kawasaki's were definite contenders for a good placing at San Jose. Needless to say, the factory Harley team with points leader Scott was in attendance.

As an indication of how hot the pace would be, Rex Beauchamp, who desperately wanted to win a mile set a 38.21 second qualifying time, an incredible 94.22 miles per hour average. Second was Keener, the winner at Syracuse and Toledo, followed by Springsteen, Lawwill and Brelsford on a Kawasaki triple. Roberts, after practising on the twin, maybe to prove to himself it wasn't fast enough, opted for the TZ, qualifying a respectable sixth.

If any of the spectators had come with any preconceived ideas of who would win, they

The 1975 Grand National season

For the last mile race at San Jose the TZ750 frame had been considerably modified but the traction problems didn't go away *(Bob Jackson)*

were quickly dispelled with the running of the four heats. Competition was fast and furious, with Brelsford winning the first heat over Beauchamp, and then Roberts high tailing it around the rail to defeat an inspired Steve Morehead and Keener. Springsteen easily won the third heat, with Castro on the other Kawasaki in fourth place, and Gary Scott was second to Mert Lawwill in the last heat.

The stage was set with both of the contenders in the final. Roberts desperately trying to stay alive, Scott having to finish in front of Roberts to claim the title. And both knowing there would be no quarter from the other riders, who were after the prize money and some of the glory. The Yamaha crew removed the badly shredded tire from the rear wheel of Roberts' bike, replacing it with an untried grooved road racing slick made by Goodyear. The conventional tire could have been turned around to provide a fresh edge to the dirt, but they all knew it wouldn't last the 25 mile final. Both riders were extremely nervous as race time approached, and in the final minutes each sat alone, getting mentally prepared for the job at hand.

It was already getting late when the riders strapped on their helmets, made sure the gloves were well down between the fingers and pushed their way to the starting line. The atmosphere was electric, with thousands of eyes riveted to the riders. Blue smoke covered the grid when everyone was finally ready with a gear selected and the clutch lever pulled back hard against the bar. The starter was the man to watch now. One second they were there, the next gone charging hard for the corner, with Lawwill in an early lead chased by Springsteen, Scott, Keener and Beauchamp. Roberts, after a fairly good start, was running competitively well until the bike began to have traction problems with the rapidly wearing untried rear tire. At one point fourth, he gradually dropped back into the pack as the problem became more acute and ironically called it a day on lap 12, when Scott was leading.

In a race that saw almost fifty lead changes in only 25 miles, Beauchamp emerged the winner, with Scott finishing fifth with a deteriorating engine. Not until he parked the bike and removed his helmet did he hear from Dick O'Brien of Robert's troubles. After three years of being second, Gary Scott had finally made it. The Number 1 plate was his.

REQUIEM FOR A TZ750 FLAT TRACKER

One week later Kenny Roberts won the Ascot Park Half mile and followed it up at the Ontario road race with the victory Gary Scott and everyone else suspected he would. With a total for the year of six victories, it was a classic example of ultimately losing the war after having won most of the battles.

The 1975 Grand National season

Gary Scott, the new Champion *(Bob Jackson)*

The 1975 Grand National season

The 1976 series was another exceptionally good racing year. 15 riders shared 28 victories and in the closest points race for years the eventual outcome of who would be Number 1 was not decided until the last race of the season at Ascot Park. The new Champion — 19 year old Jay Springsteen, a factory Harley-Davidson rider from Flint, Michigan. 'Springer' is the second youngest Grand National Champion in AMA history and his seven dirt track wins were the most since Joe Leonard won eight, in 1954.

Prior to the start of the season however, some changes had taken place. Scott could not come to terms with Harley-Davidson and decided to take a drop in salary by riding as a privateer on Harleys, Triumphs and Yamahas. Yet this wasn't the biggest bombshell, for at the end of 1975 the AMA rules committee suddenly legislated the TZ750 off the dirt tracks. The rules were changed to allow only 750cc machines with a maximum of two cylinders and this effectively eliminated the TZ and a host of other engines.

The decision was a controversial one, generating a lot of discussion from those in favor as well as those against, and it seemed for everyone who didn't want to see the machine in 1976 there was someone who did. Many enthusiasts felt sold out because the only threat to Harley-Davidson's total domination of the dirt tracks had been removed, and to them the rule change smacked of favoritism. Others argued that by allowing the TZ to run, the last vestiges of the AMA's concept of close racing on almost identical machines, where the rider made the difference, would be gone forever. Then, the riders who now could only barely afford to race would also be gone forever.

The AMA, of course, caught the heat because enthusiasts wrote in droves demanding an explanation. Some don't consider that the organization reflects the views of the people who support it, so in an effort to shed more light on the rule making procedures and the reason for the subsequent banning of the multi's, the official AMA reply to the letter writers is reproduced below word for word, with nothing omitted or taken out of context.

"I wish to thank you for taking the time to write and voice your opinion, however, I believe we should furnish you with the procedures with which rules are established.

Jay Springsteen, named Rookie of the Year, finished third in the title chase *(Bob Jackson)*

The 1975 Grand National season

Starting in 1977 novice and all lightweight classes will be returned to 250cc single cylinder, either two or four cycle engines in all types of professional competition.

Multi-cylinder motorcycles have been eliminated from professional dirt track competition for 1976, but the rule does not specifically refer to two-stroke machines. It will effect the Yamaha TZ750, the Kawasaki and Suzuki triples, as well as the four-stroke Triumph/BSA triples and the four cylinder 750cc Honda, or any 750 with more than two cylinders. Rules for professional competition are established by the professional rules committee which is defined in the AMA code of regulations. This committee includes one delegate from each class B member who manufacturers or imports the brand of motorcycle used in sanctioned competition. At present, this accounts for ten members of the committee.

Next, it includes a road race promoter, a dirt track promoter and a moto-cross promoter. These three are elected by their fellow promoters.

There are also six professional racers, some of these are elected by riders, and some earn their seats through their position in the point standings from the previous year. Likewise one professional hillclimber and two elected professional referees are included. Finally one delegate from the AMA staff, who acts as Chairman.

Basically, this committee is intended to collect opinions from all knowledgeable sources and convert these thoughts into workable rules through a democratic process. Input comes from those who promote the races, those who official (sic) the races, those who do the racing and those who build the motorcycles.

Anyone of these 23 delegates may place an item on the agenda. This item goes to the appropriate subcommittee, where it is acted upon. If it passes the subcommittee, it appears on the floor of the total committee composed of all delegates. If it passes by vote on the floor, it is recommended to the trustees of the association. The trustees may ratify, amend or overrule any action of the Professional Rules Committee.

Specifically, let's follow the rules on multi-cylinder on dirt in this procedure. At the fall of 1975 professional rules committee meeting, the proposal to limit dirt track competition to motorcycles with a maximum of two cylinders came from two sources. It was proposed by both the staff and a professional rider delegate. The proposal was assigned to the Safety and Engineering subcommittee, and was passed to the floor where it was carried. Later it was brought up for re-consideration and amended. The amendment failed 15 to 5, making the rule stand.

Finally, it was reviewed by the Board of Trustees at their next meeting and ratified, finishing its fourth round of consideration and voting, including consideration in subcommittee, in full committee, re-consideration in full committee, then by the Board of Trustees.

That's how this rule, or any professional racing rule, ends up on the books, and it is the job of the staff and the race officials to enforce it until it is changed by the same process.

Thanks for listening."

Sincerely,

W.A. Boyce
Director of Competition

WAB:bg

With 23 delegates drawn from such diverse areas of the industry - manufacturers or importers of competition machines, race promoters and riders — the theory that the majority must be Harley-Davidson supporters can be discounted. With some delegates employed by companies who import motorcycles, their allegiance is unlikely to have been directed towards Harley-Davidson, and a race promoter would have had more to gain by not banning the

The 1975 Grand National season

multis. Likewise the riders not all being Harley-Davidson mounted had no axe to grind.

What then was the reason for banning the machines? In some respects those who suggested the class C concept would be destroyed were nearer the truth, for in general it was felt that although technically wrong to ban the machines after having allowed them to race; by allowing them to continue would have increased the cost of an already expensive sport to a level which could not be tolerated. As the bikes were built basically only for mile tracks, (and even then didn't work on every type) riders who wished to remain competitive, would, by necessity, have had to build and maintain an expensive multi-cylinder machine in addition to the equipment currently used. While cost was uppermost in the minds of many, safety also concerned the rider delegates. As Gene Romero so aptly put it, "Being passed down the straight as though standing still is one thing, but going flat out into a corner and finding a TZ virtually parked up there as the guy wrestles with it is something else." In not explaining these reasons in some detail in their letter, the AMA did themselves a great disservice.

And yet, times, faces and rules do change. For instance, with more and more manufacturers producing multi-cylinder engines, where are the twins going to come from for the racers of tomorrow? The possible demise of the twin could make using multi-cylinder engines a necessity. At some time in the future the multis may yet be seen again, for the pendulum always swings both ways.

1975 AMA NATIONAL STANDINGS

		points
1.	Gary Scott	1358
2.	Kenny Roberts	1260
3.	Jay Springsteen	1027
4.	Corky Keener	929
5.	Rex Beauchamp	839
6.	Hank Scott	709
7.	Mert Lawwill	620
8.	Dave Aldana	388
9.	Gene Romero	381
10.	Greg Sassaman	335

1976 AMA NATIONAL STANDINGS*

		points
1.	Jay Springsteen	301
2.	Gary Scott	280
3.	Kenny Roberts	265
4.	Steve Eklund	141
5.	Randy Cleek	130
6.	Ted Boody	128
7.	Rex Beauchamp	125
8.	Hank Scott	118
9.	Rick Hocking	96
10.	Gene Romero	93

* In 1976 a new system of awarding points to finishers of National races was adopted

1975

Date	Event	Location	Winner	Machine	Time
1/31	25 Lap TT	Houston, Texas	Kenny Roberts	YAM	12:13.10
2/1	20 Lap ST	Houston, Texas	Darryl Hurst	YAM	5:14.72

The 1975 Grand National season

3/9	200 Mile RR	Daytona Bch, Fla.	Gene Romero	YAM	1:52:32.88
4/12	20 Lap ST	Dallas, Texas	Kenny Roberts	YAM	4:46:06
5/18	25 Mile DT (Mile)	San Jose, Ca.	Greg Sassaman	H-D	16:28.50
6/7	10 Mile DT (½ Mile)	Louisville, Ky.	Jay Springsteen	H-D	8:40.59
6/14	10 Mile DT (½ Mile)	Harrington, Del.	Jay Springsteen	H-D	9:21.09
6/22	10 Mile DT (½ Mile)	Columbus, Ohio	Gary Scott	H-D	8:50.54
7/12	25 Lap TT	Castle Rock, Wa.	Chuck Joyner	TRI	No Time
7/26	25 Lap TT	Gardena, Ca.	Gary Scott	H-D	19:49.90
8/3	75 Mile RR	Monterey, Ca.	Kenny Roberts	YAM	49:06.57
8/10	25 Lap TT	Peoria, Ill.	Sonny Burres	TRI	12:39.71
8/15	20 Lap ST	Hinsdale, Ill.	Hank Scott	YAM	6:46.52
8/17	10 Mile DT (½ Mile)	Terre Haute, Ind.	Mike Kidd	H-D	9:06.71
8/23	25 Mile DT (Mile)	Indianapolis, Ind.	Kenny Roberts	YAM	16:15.56
9/7	25 Mile DT (Mile	Syracuse, NY.	Corky Keener	H-D	15:47.17
9/13	10 Mile DT (½ Mile)	Toledo, Ohio	Corky Keener	H-D	9:53.21
9/21	25 Mile DT (Mile)	San Jose, Ca.	Rex Beauchamp	H-D	16:21.30
9/27	10 Mile DT (½ Mile)	Gardena, Ca.	Kenny Roberts	YAM	7:37.71
10/5	200 Mile RR (2x100)	Ontario, Ca.	Kenny Roberts	YAM	2:09:47.37

1976

Date	Event	Location	Winner	Machine	Time
1/23	25 Lapp TT	Houston, Texas	Rick Hocking	YAM	11:12.85
1/24	20 Lap ST	Houston, Texas	David Rush	BUL	5:03.58
3/7	200 Mile RR	Daytona Bch, Fla.	Johnny Cecotto	YAM	1:51:48.74
4/10	20 Lap ST	Dallas, Texas	Kenny Roberts	YAM	4:43.43
5/16	25 Mile DT (Mile)	San Jose, Ca.	Rex Beauchamp	H-D	15:40.02
5/23	10 Mile DT (½Mile)	Okla. City, Okla.	Hank Scott	YAM	No time †
5/29	10 Mile DT (½ Mile)	Louisville, Ky.	Gary Scott	H-D	8:43.54
6/4	20 Lap TT	Pontiac, Mich.	Steve Eklund	YAM	8:52.22
6/5	20 Lap ST	Pontiac, Mich.	Ted Boody	BUL	4:51.78
6/12	10 Mile DT (½ Mile)	Harrington, Del.	Corky Keener	H-D	8:53.88
6/20	75 Mile RR	Loudon, NH	Steve Baker	YAM	57:23.00
6/27	10 Mile DT (½ Mile)	Columbus, Ohio	Jay Springsteen	H-D	9:06.03
7/4	16 Mile DT (Mile)	Albuquerque, NM	Jay Springsteen	H-D	11:42.05**
7/10	10 Mile DT (½ Mile)	San Jose, Ca.	Kenny Roberts	YAM	8:51.26
7/17	25 Lap TT	Castle Rock, Wa.	Chuck Joyner	TRI	10:32.11
8/1	200Km. RR (2x100Km)	Monterey, Ca.	Steve Baker	YAM	1:17:06.99
8/7	25 Lap TT	Gardena, Ca.	Gary Scott	TRI	18:29.28
8/13	20 Lap TT	Hinsdale, Ill.	Steve Eklund	YAM	5:19.91
8/15	10 Mile DT (½ Mile)	Terre Haute, Ind.	Kenny Roberts	YAM	9:10.31
8/22	25 Lap TT	Peoria, Ill.	Steve Eklund	YAM	12:28.06
8/28	25 Mile DT (Mile)	Indianapolis, Ind.	Mike Kidd	H-D	15:50.32
8/29	25 Mile DT (Mile)	Indianapolis, Ind.	Jay Springsteen	H-D	No time
9/4	20 Lap ST	Talladega, Al.	Terry Poovey	BUL	No time
9/12	20 Mile DT (Mile)	Syracuse, NY	Jay Springsteen	H-D	12:18.45***
9/18	10 Mile DT (½ Mile)	Toledo, Ohio	Jay Springsteen	H-D	9:40.76
9/26	25 Mile DT (Mile)	San Jose, Ca.	Jay Springsteen	H-D	15:43.55
10/3	75 Mile RR	Riverside, Ca.	Kenny Roberts	YAM	45:03.55
10/9	10 Mile DT (½ Mile)	Gardena, Ca.	Jay Springsteen	H-D	7:36.66

† *Race red-flagged after 16 laps due to accident.*

** *Race shortened from 25 to 16 miles due to poor track conditions.*

*** *Race shortened from 25 to 20 miles due to tire-wear problems.*

The 1975 Grand National season

Though broadsliding may seem easy this is what can happen when the machine gets too far sideways and the gas is shut off *(Dan Mahony)*

8 Just turn sideways and squirt it

YOU ARE MYSTIFIED. AS SOMEONE NEW TO WATCHING THE SPORT OF FLAT TRACKING YOU CANNOT UNDERSTAND WHY THE RIDING STYLE OF TODAY'S RACE VARIED SO MUCH FROM THAT OF THE PREVIOUS WEEK. THEN THE RIDERS WERE SLIDING SIDEWAYS THROUGH THE CORNERS, BUT TODAY THEY SEEMED TO BE TRACKING AS THOUGH ON RAILS. THE REASON — THE TYPE OF SURFACE AND LAYOUT OF THE RACE TRACKS. WHILE THEY MAY LOOK IDENTICAL FROM GROUND LEVEL, MANY DIFFER IN SURFACE AND LAYOUT AND HENCE CANNOT BE RIDDEN IN THE SAME MANNER.

As any professional who competes in events around the country will testify, there is no set standardization as regards the length of the straights and radii of the corners for mile and half mile tracks. Maybe seventy percent are what could be described as normal, with the straights being in proportion to the circumference of the corners, but others are definite oddballs. Some are more or less round, like Louisville, Kentucky, with virtually no straight to speak of, while others, like Salem, Oregon, have ultra long straights connected to two U-turns at either end. In addition to the layout, the width of the racetracks vary considerably.

Surfaces also play a major part in how riders attack the race track. There are two distinct types, plus a combination of both.

A track with a hard, dry, smooth surface on which rubber from the tires is laid down is called 'grooved', 'blue grooved', or 'notched' depending upon which area of the country a rider might be from. The groove appears during practice as a black strip around the racetrack, and varies in width from as little as one foot wide to a maximum of two or three. There is little choice but for everyone to ride the groove as this is where the traction is; any loose dirt displaced will have been thrown to either side, and anyone who deviates from the rubber by virtue of misjudging his entry speed into the corner will instantly lose places, for the grip on either side is akin to riding on marbles.

The cushion track on the other hand has a loose, even surface, which varies anywhere from ½ in. to 3 in. thickness. Though displaced by the sideways motion of the wheels, it is pulled back and levelled by a grading machine prior to each race. The advantage of a cushion track is that there is usually more than one racing line through the corners; the more daring leave the throttle on longer into the corner, sliding high around the fence, while others shutting off sooner slide a slightly lower, yet shorter, route.

The combination of a grooved and cushioned track is the result of a cushioned track which is not graded in between races. The track starts the day cushioned, later becomes grooved and cushioned at the same time, and then finishes up the day being a grooved track only. As the dirt from the inside line is thrown out, it is not replaced, and a groove forms on the hard pack

Just turn sideways and squirt it

Above South Bay near San Diego is a good example of a grooved track. Here a rider keeps front and rear wheels in as near line astern as possible, following the radius of the corner *(Author)*

Below Loose even surfaced cushion tracks are where all those breathtakingly spectacular shots are taken. Here Mark Brelsford really gets it on *(Dan Mahony)*

below. Meantime, the cushion around the fence has been replaced with dirt from the inside line, but even this disappears as the day wears on, and everyone is relegated to the groove as the quickest way through the corner.

As can be imagined, these differing track surfaces require different techniques, which is why riders can be seen sliding one week and riding as though on rails the next. On the narrow grooved tracks front and rear wheels are generally kept as nearly as possible in line astern, while on a deep cushion the motorcycle will be completely sideways under full throttle. Variations in the width of the groove or depth of the cushion also show up as more or less sideways action, and in some instances where the track conditions change throughout the day, the rider has by necessity to adjust his style and lines from practice, through qualifying, to racing.

As the corners of the deep cushioned track, which incidentally is where all those spectacular broadsliding photographs are taken, offers probably the greatest challenge, these will be dealt with in as much general detail as the relatively few seconds negotiating them allow. All other racetracks require the technique to a lesser extent (or maybe not at all as in the case of a narrow groove) hence covering them would only be duplication, and would add confusion to an already difficult subject.

Before getting to it, however, there are some other important aspects to be discussed which go into ensuring fast lap times.

Reference has been made previously to the braking system fitted to flat track machines and probably now is a good time to express some thoughts on the subject.

With speeds down the straight (and into the corners) ever increasing over the years, the AMA rules committee felt that all riders, whether novice, junior or expert, should have the option of fitting and using, as necessary, a rear wheel braking system. Though many of the better experts felt the device unnecessary (having learnt their craft on machines that couldn't be braked mechanically and over the years had adjusted to the higher speeds) they fitted it as a precautionary measure against any emergency that might arise, such as avoiding a fallen rider or preventing a shunt if closely following behind someone who uses the brake. There is little fear of the latter occurring at National events, but in non-National events around the country the visitor unfamiliar with the local way of doing things must be prepared for the possibility.

There is one other instance where the brake is of value. If by misjudging his entry speed a rider finds himself slipping off the narrow rubber strip of a grooved track, the slide can be arrested by 'tapping' the brake lever and the machine gathered back onto the groove.

While there is a definite feeling by the majority of experts against the need for brakes, the AMA specifically requires them for amateur competition (Chapter 9 — Buying a Bike). The prime reason, naturally enough, is safety, but the ranks of the professionals are filled from those of the amateurs and unfortunately for the amateur the trend in professional racing is away from using brakes. The amateur has either to learn not to use the brake from when he takes up racing, or to stop using it when sufficiently confident and experienced. Of the two methods, the first is probably the least painful and the amateur who adopts it invariably becomes the better rider.

How often has it been said that the best riders become one with their machines? Possibly thousands of times, but it is true. There are many items on a racing motorcycle with which the rider must be attuned, for they can have tremendous effect on his performance, but once a workable combination is found, very few of the top professionals deviate from that combination. In general, there are only two items changed from race track to race track — gearing and tires. Occasionally, rear shock springs might be clicked up a notch, or the front forks pushed down slightly through the triple clamps, for extremely rough tracks. However, this is the limit to which most will usually go with suspension.

When gearing a motorcycle for either mile or half mile tracks, a sprocket for the rear wheel must be chosen which allows the engine to deliver its maximum horsepower on the fastest part of the circuit. This point on oval tracks is at the end of the straights, just prior to shutting off for the corners. The machine is then geared one tooth higher as under 'combat' conditions the rider will be trying harder and thus peak power would be achieved before the fastest point is reached.

Just turn sideways and squirt it

Goodyear's D/T II mile tire *(Author)*

Further modification to the gearing might be necessary if the rider finds the machine over-geared for the corners, and then most will consider a trade off — properly geared for the corners, slightly undergeared for the straights — as long as the overall gain in time is greater than the loss.

Because of new compounds recently developed resulting in a totally new Goodyear tire, type D/T II, the practise of keeping handy a pile of different tires for varying conditions on mile tracks has virtually ended. For as many years as can be remembered, it has been normal to lug around a selection of tires, which included Goodyear, Pirelli, Dunlop, and Carlisle, but the Goodyear D/T II has almost overnight made obsolete the vast majority. On half mile tracks there is still a need to use different types of tires for different surfaces, though this situation will probably also change when Goodyear produces a half mile tire. Sometime during the 1977 season is the time given as the introduction date, according to those with an ear to the ground.

In the grip department, the Goodyear D/T II is the difference between night and day when compared to any other tire. It very quickly hooks up to the ground under hard acceleration and obtains tremendous sidebite when broadsliding through corners.

With the motorcycle set up, let's look at what is involved in getting around a cushioned mile and half mile track.

The start is important, as it is in most racing, but with relatively short races the stops have to be pulled out immediately and a good bite off the line is essential. From a sitting position the upper body weight is placed forward over the handlebars, to prevent huge wheelies, and the throttle rolled on to ensure the tire bites at the ground. Snapping open the throttle usually results in power that should be giving traction going up in smoke and wheelspin. On mile tracks, riders start in low gear, half mile tracks in second gear. As soon as top gear is selected, the gear lever is forgotten about until the end of the race. The throttle, left leg and shifting body weight are the sole controlling factors involved.

Although all of the motions of cornering can be gone through in the text, the one ingredient that cannot come through is the very high speeds at which these motorcycles travel. On a mile or half mile track, maximum speed is attained at the end of the straight and held thru part of the corner. For a mile, this is around 132mph, with a lap average of 95mph. In the case of a half mile, 91mph and 70mph.

Just turn sideways and squirt it

Above At the start body weight should be positioned forward to prevent wheelies off the line *(Author)*

Below *Figure 2.* The way around a mile cushioned track *(Author)*

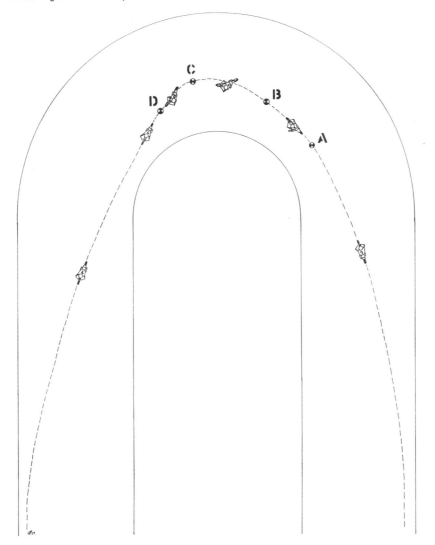

Just turn sideways and squirt it

The art of cornering on a cushion type track is to make the straights as long as possible, then turn once, acutely, rather than the two or three times needed if the corner were adhered to as a 180 degree turn.

Figure 2 shows a hypothetical racetrack on which the dotted line represents the path a motorcycle will take. At point A at maximum speed, the rider shuts off the throttle while at the same time pulling his weight forward and inboard towards the gas tank, putting his left leg down on the ground and making sure the right boot is positioned to help lever the back end of the machine around. There is no real effort involved for the right leg and foot as the footrest is positioned lower and further to the rear than on a normal road going motorcycle. The action of shutting off the throttle and redistributing the weight induces the bike to start drifting outwards along the chosen line. When the throttle, the only method of controlling the machine, is closed, both rider and machine are literally out of control from point A to point B.

B is the point where the men are sorted out from the boys, for this is where the throttle must be rolled back on. The closer the distance between B and C, the more speed that will have been lost which cannot then be made back up. The closer B is to A the lower the lap time, but it takes an extremely confident and forceful rider to get back on the throttle so early when the motorcycle still has so much momentum. When the throttle is cracked back on at point B, the rear end will hang out, but in some circumstances the rider may have to induce it to hang out by using either the biggest lever he has — his leg — or maybe by an involuntary flicking of the hips. By applying more throttle, balancing the motorcycle on his left leg, and steering along the chosen curve, the rider holds the broadsliding position until position C, which is the transition point from going sideways to again going forwards. The rear tire though going sideways during this time is gripping (sidebite) the racetrack thru the sidewalls.

Although C is marked as a definite point, at no actual fixed point does the motorcycle cease going sideways to suddenly commence going forward. Both motions blend together in a curve around the apex of the turn. However, one definite action at point C begins to send the motorcycle off in a forward direction sooner than if left to its own devices and is the mark of a better than normal rider, for not everyone can do it. The handlebars are turned inwards towards the exit of the corner.

Just in case the whole process appears too easy on paper, remember that loss of grip, too much grip, rough spots or slick spots thru any part of the corner can result in the rider being flicked over the top of the machine (highsiding) or sliding to the ground (lowsiding).

At point D the rider will be back on full throttle getting bite from the race track. He may still be leaning slightly from the vertical but both feet will be back on the pegs, body weight will have been moved to the rear of the seat to induce grip, and fifty feet will have been added to the length of the straight.

On mile courses, with drafting playing an important part, he will tuck down as soon as possible to cheat the wind, and if not leading will probably move in behind someone to catch a tow down the long straights, unless of course, the intention is to overtake. Depending on the situation, the throttle may either be kept fully open, or eased off slightly if the rider is content to hold his position. Positioning is of prime importance because the majority of races are won or lost from the last corner to the finish line, and no one wants to be in first position going into the last lap unless he has a commanding lead, for chances are someone drafting will pull out just prior to the finish and take the flag. Though some more inexperienced riders draft on half mile courses, there is no advantage, as the straights are simply not long enough to attain sufficient speed.

A final note on spills. Highsiding over the motorcycle happens so quickly with virtually no warning that preparing for it is impossible; however, with lowsiding there are two schools of thought. Some like to stay with the machine while others abandon it. Gene Romero opts for the first measure for two reasons. The motorcycle eats up the racetrack instead of him doing so, and one object is easier for the closely following riders to miss than two. The white leathers Gene wears are also a safety feature as either with the machine or separated from it, he is easily noticeable.

Just turn sideways and squirt it

Above At point A the rider shuts off the gas, pulls his weight forward and inboard, and puts his foot down *(Bob Jackson)*

Below The leading rider in this shot is back on the gas at point B which in part puts the motorcycle into the broadsliding position. The second rider is not quite there yet *(Bob Jackson)*

Just turn sideways and squirt it

Above Jay Springsteen always gets back on the gas early wasting as little time as possible *(Dan Mahony)*

Below Rex Beauchamp at the absolute limit before making the transition from sideways to forward motion at point C *(Dan Mahony)*

Just turn sideways and squirt it

Above Three riders between points C and D (see Figure 2) illustrate graphically how the broadsiding motion blends into forward motion around the apex of the corner. Kenny Roberts (2) and Jay Springsteen (25) with their feet back on the pegs have reached point D; Steve Morehead is almost there *(Dan Mahony)*

Below Drafting plays an essential part down the long straights of mile tracks especially for those riders down on horsepower whose only hope of hanging on is to be sucked along with the faster machines *(Bob Jackson)*

Just turn sideways and squirt it

Above Riding too close to the hay bales doesn't leave room for mistakes. This rider with no warning of impending disaster had no options open to him *(Dan Mahony)*

Below Lowsiding after losing the front end. Stay with the bike or kick it away? *(Dan Mahony)*

9 Come slide with us

'I WANT TO RACE, BUT HOW DO I START?' AN OFTEN HEARD QUESTION TO WHICH FINDING THE ANSWER WHEN NOT IN THE KNOW CAN PROVE DIFFICULT. TO THE MANY POTENTIAL FLAT TRACKERS OUT THERE, WHOSE INTEREST HAS BEEN SPARKED THROUGH WHATEVER REASON, HERE ARE SOME ANSWERS WHICH SHOULD AT LEAST POINT YOU IN THE RIGHT DIRECTION.

If you should ask any of the top professionals where they got their early dirt track experience, the odds are pretty much loaded towards the answer being 'in amateur competition.' Becoming proficient in amateur racing is the first step to obtaining a novice, then a junior and ultimately an expert professional license.

One of the beauties of amateur competition is that it allows you to proceed at your own pace, riding against only those of your own ability. Like the professionals, you will start at the bottom as a novice, racing for trophies and/or merchandise prizes valued at less than $100 (£60) per prize award, and continue upwards, through junior to expert status, at which stage you will be allowed to compete in semi-professional meets where the prize money is limited to $600 (£360) total. Amateur riders wishing to maintain their amateur status may accept trophies rather than cash.

After achieving expert amateur status (also known as A class rating, with juniors B and novices C) you may want to move on to become a novice professional. No one will insist you lose your amateur status, that decision is entirely up to you. Many hundreds do make the transition and some go onto greater things, but it is worthwhile remembering that unless you are exceptionally good, you will probably go from the top of the heap to the bottom again. This happens in all sports. For instance, consider the star college football player who becomes a professional. All of a sudden he is just one of the guys again, doing nothing spectacular, and some can't handle that. But first things first.

To prepare riders for half-mile racing, races are held in many areas of the country, on shorter tracks. In short track racing, with much shorter straights, lap speeds are slower and this type of track is ideal for the beginner. With only a limited number of half mile tracks in his native Texas, Mike Kidd came up through the ranks of amateur competition by short track racing, an extremely popular branch of the sport in the Lone Star State. His ability now makes him one of the best short track racers in the country, yet it in no way detracts from his performance on half mile and mile courses. It is simply a natural progression to move onto bigger things and the experience and confidence gained makes the transition to half mile and ultimately mile racing easier than at first imaginable. The other plus, of course, with starting on short tracks, is that should your ultimate goal be to earn your living by racing professionally, you will have mastered already an art which forms a part of professional racing.

Another type of amateur competition which is popular are TT scrambles. This type of event is similar to a TT but with the course being as little as a quarter mile in length or as long as two

Come slide with us

Bill Oliver *(Bob Jackson)*

miles. Irregular left and right turns, plus a jump, make this type of racing sound tutoring in machine handling. Should you think this kind of event has no value, consider what it did for the career of Gene Romero, who, at fourteen years of age, became Central California's 250cc amateur scrambles champ.

By riding in events, you will become proficient at sliding a machine, but it is advantageous to have learnt beforehand. On the track you can refine the art, no doubt finishing up on your backside a few times before having mastered it, or knowing just how far you can push it. With most riders living in the cities and racetracks not available for practise, one question has to be 'Where can I learn to do this?' The answer isn't simple, although it might have been twenty or thirty years ago, when more open spaces were available. There are motorcycle parks which admittedly cater more to motocross and play riders, but some have a short track which can be used. At the least there will be a large flat open area where you can practise. If there is no park there are always either the dry lakes for the inhabitants of the southwest or fields and meadows in the midwest and east. Dry lakes don't usually require permission to use, as they are government (read people) owned, but a farmer's meadow will. Failing these two alternatives, dirt roads away from the madding crowd can provide some instruction but be prepared for the local gendarmerie. In case of emergencies have your escape route worked out well in advance where cars cannot follow (And don't forget to weave!!).

As it is nationwide and generally accepted as THE organization for motorcyclists, all information pertains only to the AMA. But already someone has jumped up to protest. Okay, the AMA is not the only game in town, for across the country races for amateurs (and professionals) are run under the auspices of organizations unknown outside of a particular area or state, and many do an excellent job.

There are many reasons as to why these other organizations exist. It is argued the AMA is too large and because it controls all forms of motorcycle racing, plus looking after the interests of street riders, it is not in tune with any particular form of racing. The debate goes on, but as the AMA has been around for fifty years it must be doing something right, and with its grip on the sport, no doubt will still be around in another fifty.

Though not without its faults, the AMA has served its members pretty well over the years. It brought American motorcycling out of the dark ages to a point where it is now respected as a legitimate sport. (Credit must also go to Bruce Brown, whose full length feature film *On*

Come slide with us

Any Sunday, released in the early seventies, did much to improve the image of the motorcycle racer and motorcycle racing). Should you start with another organisation at some time you will come into contact with the AMA, for if it is the best guys you want to race against, they are all into AMA racing.

For ease of administration, the AMA splits the country into various districts, with each semi autonomous, running its own affairs under the overall direction of AMA headquarters. Clubs abound in every district and most of the amateur competition is run by these clubs. Dates for every type of event are formulated early in the year and usually also publicized before race date in local and regional motorcycle papers. Naturally, to take part in this type of competition, you have to be a member of the AMA. An application form can usually be found on the counter of most motorcycle stores or is obtainable from the: American Motorcycle Association, PO Box 141, Westerville, Ohio 43081. On receipt of $12 (£7) you will be issued with a membership card which resembles a credit card, plus an *Amateur and Semi Professional Rule Book.* Membership also entitles you to voting privileges when election time for officials rolls around. You will be informed of whom to write in your district for a racing number and that basically is the limit of the paperwork.

As with the professionals, you are required to supply notarized parental consent to the local district if under the age of majority in your state, so in passing, a few words about parents. They have your best interests at heart, but in most cases are uninformed about motorcycle racing, which can result in their denying you permission to race. Talk to them, take them to races, try desparately to get them interested, for opinions and preconceived ideas can change. You may even be surprised to find they enjoy it, in which case any ulterior motives you may have for interesting them (such as sounding out the Old Man for a few bucks to help finance an expensive sport) may be negated by, dare it be said, his spontaneous offer to help.

Starting from scratch with no friends in racing can have its problems, as for a while you feel like an outsider unable to penetrate the inner ring. Friends are there if you look and many will be more than ready to help with much of the information you need to know. A local AMA

The AMA's district and regional map *(The AMA)*

Come slide with us

chartered club is probably one of the best sources of information for the newcomer, while the right motorcycle store can also be a haven of information. Cultivate a friendship with a dealer who sponsors or employs riders. Only one in ten thousand will ever turn you away as most realise a friendship will be mutually rewarding. The prospective rider gets his information and invariably orders parts or accessories from the dealer. So don't hang back — ask questions. You need all the help you can get, and besides, good friends are worth their weight in gold.

If at all possible, try to take someone at least a little knowledgeable about the sport along with you to the races, for as mentioned, there is a lot to learn, and just being there the first few times is confusing enough. Having a friend around who you can talk to, can monitor your efforts out on the track, and offer some constructive criticism, will make life more pleasant and the racing more enjoyable. After all that's why you want to race!

Are you ready to go out and buy a bike?

BUYING A BIKE

In amateur dirt track and short track events classes exist as follows:

Class	Engine Size
1	0 to 100cc
2	101 to 125cc
3	126 to 175cc
4	176 to 200 cc
5	201 to 250cc (except two-stroke multi cylinder engines)
6	201 to 250cc two-stroke multi-cylinder engines
7	251 to 360cc all other types

Not all classes are necessarily run if advertised in advance, and some districts may have supplemental regulations, which allow larger equipment.

Those with a sharp eye will have already noticed that apart from the inclusion of the smaller classes, class 6 does not match the type of equipment used in professional racing. Class 6 was the original equipment ruling for the novice professional on half miles, and experts on short tracks, prior to January 1, 1977. As the amateur arm of the sport follows very closely the rules and regulations of professional racing, and must be considered the next logical step upwards for the serious rider, why wasn't the engine limitation changed for amateurs, considering the professional ruling was changed in the interests of safety?

Maybe a simple answer is that the rule change has scrapped a lot of engines in professional racing, and in an effort not to force amateurs out of the sport, it was decided to keep the rules as they were. Also the speeds attained in amateur racing are lower and consequently safer to begin with.

'With all those classes, what displacement bike should I ride?' The answer can only be whatever the rider feels happy with. Younger riders might want to start with under 250cc machines but for the older rider, a 250cc single cylinder machine (class 5) should fit the bill perfectly. In this class you will learn to ride a bike the pros use, which can only be an asset, and you can be competitive at a reasonable cost.

A choice will have to be made between a two-stroke or four-stroke engine, but for a beginner this may be the least of his worries, for having raced neither, no preference would exist.

In general, a two-stroke will be lighter because it contains fewer moving parts, though harder to learn to ride because the usable power is delivered over a narrower range of rpm. The four-stroke engine has a much more forgiving nature, with power over a much broader range, but its development has not kept pace with the two-stroke. However, do not confuse outright horsepower with low lap times, for although related, they are not necessarily compatible. A moderately tuned reliable four-stroke can be as effective a tool as a high revving, narrow power banded two-stroke, on which the rider has difficulty using and putting the horses to the ground.

Come slide with us

As a beginner, your first consideration should be a reliable (yet relatively quick) machine, for nothing is more disillusioning than an ultra trick bike which is beyond your riding capabilities. Can you remember learning to drive a car? Everything seemed to be happening at once; there was no time to relax. Well that's how it is going to be until you feel comfortable on the race track. Don't compound the problem by buying a motorcycle you cannot ride. There will be lots of time to experiment later.

As bikes built from scratch outnumber the commercially available race bikes, a prospective buyer cannot sit down with a bunch of brochures, trying to get some idea of what to buy and how much to pay. As of writing there are four complete commercially available machines you might want to consider — the Bultaco Astro, Champion-Can-Am, Champion-KTM, and Ossa ST-1. However, buying either a used one of these or a used bike built from scratch may be the best way to go for a number of reasons:

1. A used bike will be ready to go, requiring very little set up, something worth considering should your technical knowledge be batting zero at this point.
2. Spares such as sprockets and even engine parts may be included in the deal, especially if the seller is moving up to a larger machine.
3. A bike is not the only consideration at this point as many other things will also be needed, and a used bike will probably fit your budget far better than buying new or building from scratch.
4. It is possible (and no disgrace) to discover after your first few outings that this type of racing is not your bag, in which case the resale value of the bike will not have dropped as dramatically as would a new or custom-made machine.

Begin a search for a used machine in the classified ads of motorcycle papers, or ask around at club meetings to find what is for sale. Comparing various machines will give you some idea of price but be prepared to pay in the region of $1,500 (£900) for a clean, well prepared and well taken care of machine. Bikes of less than 250cc capacity should be cheaper. The types of frames, wheels, forks etc. used are covered in a previous chapter and knowing the various separate prices of these items will help evaluate the overall asking price.

When shopping for a bike, having someone along who races or knows what to look for is a great asset, and this kind of help cannot be over emphasised. Some dealers who are into the sport will sometimes know of, or have a machine for sale, and most reputable dealers will offer some sort of guarantee should you buy from them. In general, don't settle for the first bike you see. Shop around and if at all possible try to arrange a test ride.

Don't be afraid to ask questions if considering a particular bike. Most owners will usually tell what idiosyncrasies a bike has and what parts give trouble, if any. As most are tuned, engine manual information is only useful for identifying and putting parts back in the right order, so try to find out as much as possible. It could save you a lot of headaches sometime in the future.

Any machine used in AMA competition will have met the rules regarding legality, but reading the AMA Amateur and Semi-Professional Rule Book section on equipment could be advantageous when buying a machine. For example, the majority of machines will be found to have a rear brake, while a few may not. The brake, usually a disc type, is not mandatory in professional racing but is for amateurs, and buying a machine without a rear brake will result in having to go out and buy all the pieces. So check for what is and isn't required.

Most other safety features are now universally accepted for most types of racing but are worth mentioning in passing. All motorcycles must be equipped with a self-closing throttle and a kill button, mounted on the left handlebar. All drain plugs must be lock or safety wired, primary drives enclosed, and control levers ball ended. Footpegs must also fold back at forty five degrees and be covered with at least one quarter inch of rubber or plastic. In the interests of better public relations all machines have to be muffled.

NOTE!

California has enacted legislation which requires every competition or off road motorcycle　**127**

Come slide with us

either be licensed for the street, or licensed for use on public lands and trails only at an annual fee of $15 (£9), or taxed at a one time rate of $3 (£2) if transported to, and used solely on closed circuit race tracks! Non compliance results in a fine if stopped for some other traffic violation, so check your state regulations before venturing out onto the highway with your seemingly innocent racing machine.

RIDING APPAREL

The US has done its share over the years in bringing color to motorcycle racing and the sport is better for it. Previously attired in black, the riders of yesteryear were almost indistinguishable from each other, but this situation has changed, with multi colored leathers and helmets being universally worn by all.

Buying a wardrobe should not be treated lightly, for an ill-fitting helmet or badly tailored leathers can make one feel so uncomfortable it becomes impossible to concentrate on the job at hand. Even if you are an impatient person by nature, be prepared to spend time getting the right fit.

The only other consideration when buying racing attire is to remember its prime purpose. While you are on the bike it serves no other purpose than keeping the wind off, or maybe keeping you warm. However, its a whole different ball game should you fall for the helmet and clothing are the only protection you have. Sliding on your backside for ten yards can be painful enough, more especially so if the first five yards have worn through the seat of your el cheapo leathers. Quality costs money, doesn't your body deserve it?

Motorcycle racers, like competitors in other sports, tend to gravitate to the companies which produce the best of whatever it is they wish to buy. Some companies, such as Bell (the helmet people), are known the world over, and one of the reasons for successes like these is an uncompromising attitude towards producing quality products on which the buyer can depend. While no endorsement of any product is intended, the companies mentioned are the ones from which flat trackers tend to buy.

Helmet

No one should compromise where the safety of his head is concerned, which is probably why many racers prefer a Bell helmet over a variety of less expensive, but still legally safe helmets.

Preference for style is up to the rider, and for everyone who choses a full coverage model, an equal number prefer the open face or space type helmet. What type of helmet should you buy? There again it is all a matter of personal preference, but be prepared to pay up to $65 (£40) for the full coverage models. Try on both styles and base your choice on what feels comfortable; there is no other way.

Whatever make or style helmet you choose, make sure it has the approved stickers of either the Snell Foundation or US Department of Transportation, as this is your guarantee the helmet has met, and can meet, certain standards of punishment.

Eye Protection

All riders are required to wear some form of eye protection. Fixed face shields on open face helmets, and flip shields on full coverage helmets, are the most popular in this type of racing. For longer races, tearaway lenses are usually taped around either type shield and then ripped away as the dirt builds up and obscures vision. Most goggles have no provision for taping on extra lenses and those that have don't offer the lower face protection rider's prefer.

Helmets come with provision for attaching either a flip or fixed face shield and it is a simple matter to learn how to tape on tearaways for the longer races, where dirt is a problem. Watch someone do it if you are unsure of how, for most have it down to a fine art whereby a small amount of tape is used, requiring only a minimum of effort to rip off.

Discarded tearaways can usually be found lying around the pits or the edge of the race track but they will be scratched and unworthy of your attention. Made from acetate, they scratch fairly easily, making vision difficult, so take care when cleaning.

What the well dressed flat tracker is wearing; helmet with integral face shield, boots, skid shoe, and gloves (Author)

Above Two examples of head protection; the Bell Star and Super Magnum

When taping on tearoffs use a minimum of tape to ensure that the lens can be ripped off quickly and with little effort (Bob Jackson)

Come slide with us

Superman in hot pursuit of a telephone booth? No, just Dave Aldana showing some of the variety that has brightened racing leathers in recent years *(Bob Jackson)*

Come slide with us

Leathers

A set of leathers is probably the most expensive piece of clothing any racer owns, and a beginner can expect to pay at least $150 (£90) for a custom set. Although initially expensive, leathers will last for a good many years provided they are looked after, and don't spend too much time sliding along the ground with someone inside them.

Many companies produce leathers and good ones at that, but two names continually crop up whenever flat track leathers are mentioned — Bates and ABC. It doesn't matter if you live on the other side of the country from either of these two companies, for ordering can be done by mail. On the face of it, this admittedly sounds risky when ordering a custom-made item but really isn't because every eventuality is covered, and you will be dealing with a reputable company. The customer receives an order form showing the measurements required, with instructions and diagrams on how to obtain certain measurements. You will need someone to handle the tape measure and most mothers, wives or girl friends usually know enough about sewing to avoid any serious mistakes.

Flat track leathers are made in two pieces, pants and a jacket or vest coming together at the waist. One piece leathers do not give the flexibility needed to clamber around the bike and an added advantage is that the jacket can be removed inbetween races, a real boon on a hot day.

Getting one's first set of leathers is always an ego trip, so savor the moment. Crouch down (as though sitting on a bike) and check there is enough room in the seat, at the knees and the elbows. A set of leathers which only fits in a standing position will do nothing for you on a bike. Those colors staring at you in the mirror may seem bright now but hardly anyone will notice you in the pits, and the newness will soon wear off. Turn around, there's your name stitched on the back just below the shoulder line above the number assigned you by the district. Makes you feel good doesn't it?

Boots and a Skid Shoe

The choice of boots is whatever you feel comfortable in, for the only stipulation is that they be 8 in or more high. Many riders opt for lace up boots while others prefer the buckled motocross variety. Whichever type of boots you choose, a steel skid shoe will have to be fabricated to fit the left boot — the one on which the bike is balanced while sliding around corners. Having a well fitted steel shoe tailored for the type of track you are riding on can make a big difference in performance, for the resistance between the boot and the ground will be reduced, permitting better control of the machine.

Ken Maely, known to everyone in the sport as 'The Shoe Man' has been making steel shoes for amateur and professional dirt track riders since 1950. He is the acknowledged expert on the subject, indeed it seems he is the only person engaged in this type of business in the United States. The chances are if this is your sport, Maely will make your steel shoe too.

Each shoe is custom-made to each boot, the sole being made from annealed band saw blade with a hard alloy facing welded to it after the stamped mild steel toecap and heel piece are welded in place. When ordering, it is only necessary to state what kind of racing you will be doing, plus of course send the left boot. Short tracks, tight scrambles or courses where the surface is rough and loose will require a shoe with a rounded bottom, curved up at the front. For smooth hard half miles the shoe should be slightly curved at the front and on the inside edge, while milers use a flat bottomed shoe with only a minimum of curve at the front and inside edge.

In order to keep the toe pointing upwards, thus ensuring the shoe planes across the surface, the heel should be removed from the left boot.

Unless your feet grow, a steel shoe should last for many years, and even when the hard facing on the sole is worn down after two to five years of racing, it can be returned to Maely to be built up yet again. The cost of a new steel shoe is about $45 (£25) which, when broken down over a number of years, works out at only a few dollars a year.

Gloves

Although there is no stipulation in the rules that riders must wear gloves, the majority do.

Come slide with us

Left Ken Maely — the shoe man — is well known around the National circuit. Here he resurfaces a steel shoe in the pits prior to a day's racing *(Author)*

Below Having a correctly fitted steel shoe, made especially for the type of track to be ridden on makes a big difference — sometimes between winning and losing *(Bob Jackson)*

Any kind will suffice though soft, thin leather motocross gloves are the most popular.

Protective Equipment
Although used extensively in motocross, protective equipment hasn't found much of a following among flat track racers, but shin and knee guards and occasionally chest protectors are sometimes used.

Rocks or wet clumps of earth are thrown back on some racetracks and riders wearing short boots usually opt for Jim Davis shin and knee guards to protect their lower legs. Only when the debris is really flying will chest protectors be brought out, as the majority of leathers, padded in the chest area, provide sufficient protection under more normal conditions.

Apart from absorbing the sting of a missile, shin and knee guards, or any other piece of protective equipment, is of limited value in this type of racing, because falls generally occur at the corners when the wheels lose all traction and the rider slides a short distance to the ground. At seventy miles an hour in a situation such as this most protective equipment is of little use, unless it is strapped to the rider's backside.

Tools
Riding week after week you will soon become familiar with your bike's needs, learning its little idiosyncrasies, finding which parts need constant attention or adjustment, and in general amassing a surprising amount of knowledge. However, to do all this you are going to need tools — lots of 'em. It is impossible to say exactly what tools for everyone has their own ideas of what comprises a tool kit, but there are basics needed which can be added to as you become more knowledgeable and attack more serious problems.

First and foremost consider buying a tool chest. Why a chest and not a tool box? For one very good reason. The pit area at most meets is within the infield, which necessitates the vehicles being removed to allow sufficient room for all, and the spectators to see the racing all around the track. Should additional tools which cannot be stuffed into a tool box be needed, a walk to the parking lot is in order, and that may be difficult if a race is in progress and you need a special tool to complete a job before the next race — your race. Of course tools which don't fit in the box can be left on the ground but they usually finish up being lost in the dirt, or heaven forbid, stolen.

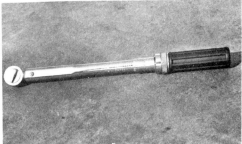

Above With no pointer or dial to watch, this type torque wrench is a breeze to use. Simply set the torque required on the micrometer type barrel and a loud 'click, click' is heard when the correct tightness is reached *(Author)*

Left A tool chest large enough to hold every tool which may be needed on race day is essential *(Author)*

Come slide with us

A compartmentalized tool chest has enough space for storage of differing sets of wrenches, with the hinged top area sufficient to hold hammers and larger odd shaped tools. Probably the best known and used type is one sold by Sears Roebuck, which is the top half of a two piece unit; the bottom section contains larger compartments and with its rubber wheels can be rolled around a garage or working area to where needed. Either piece can be purchased separately, a nice convenience as you may never need the larger portable unit.

Next on the list are wrenches and sockets. Again Sears Craftsman tools are highly respected with a large selection on view, supermarket style, at most Sears stores across the country. A basic tool kit ought to include a set of open end wrenches, box (ring) wrenches, and a socket set, but your purchases may have to be doubled if your engine is imported and the cycle parts are made in the USA. We are slowly edging towards adopting the metric system but until we do, the problem of differing thread systems will continue to be a hassle, with domestic nuts and bolts requiring one set of wrenches while the vast majority of imported items need metric.

Open ended wrenches tend to be 'low man on the totem pole' compared to sockets or boxes which are usually quicker and don't slip; yet there are always tight spots where only open ended wrenches can be used. Box wrenches, because of their offset handles, are easier to use, sparing knuckles, and work well with sockets at removing nuts. Most socket sets are available with numerous extension pieces, universal joints, and drives which can make life a lot easier. Many nuts and bolts hidden away among the frame tubes can be removed very simply and quickly, provided the right attachment is at hand.

If you are starting from scratch trying to become a proficient mechanic, you will at some time strip a thread or break a bolt by tightening it too tight. This will probably take place on a Saturday evening, the bolt will invariably be of the cylinder head variety, and your friendly local motorcycle dealer will have closed hours ago. At times like these you will yearn for a torque wrench.

This clever but simple tool enables patterns of bolts to be tightened down evenly to a predetermined setting without fear of a leak (gas pressure from within the cylinder) or worse still, the dreaded stripping. Torque is simply a measure of force (the strength of your arm) multiplied by the distance over which the force is applied (the length of the wrench) and is usually measured in foot pounds (ft. lb.) Hence it is easily seen that 50lb. applied to the end of a wrench 1ft. long will result in 50 ft. lb. of torque having been applied to the bolt.

Many mechanics will argue they can 'feel' the right amount of torque to be applied to a bolt with an ordinary wrench, while some can, the majority cannot. Granted working every day on engines does give the career mechanic a definite advantage, for he develops a rapport with his tools. But the old saying of familiarity breeding contempt still holds true. A torque wrench is one of the most singularly expensive tools an amateur mechanic will ever buy; however the cost is easily justifiable for it doesn't take many heli-coil jobs to equal the initial purchase price.

What type of torque wrench to buy? The preference seems to lie with the 'click, click' type as it is by far the easiest to use. There are no pointers or dials to watch, the torque required is simply set on a micrometer type barrel at the end of the shaft. When the correct torque has been applied to the bolt, a loud 'click, click' is heard. Many automobile parts stores (and Sears) sell this type of wrench and though more expensive than either the pointer or dial face type, it has become a favorite of amateur and professional mechanics alike.

Wrenches are the basic ingredient of any tool kit but like a recipe, many other items have to be added (although not necessarily all at once) to complete the whole thing.

One tool which should not be left out is a hammer, for hammers can do wondrous things when all else fails. Available in all shapes and sizes, an ideal type is a 2lb. ball and peen. The flat hitting face is usually large enough to make it almost impossible to miss whatever is swung at, while the peen or rounded end can often be used to advantage where space is limited. To complement the hammer, a hide or rubber mallet is useful in helping to remove parts which cannot be damaged. Given time, you will probably be adjusting gearing by swapping rear wheel sprockets and a mallet is a useful aid in removing spindles, the threads of which do not respond well to hammer blows.

Crosshead screws found in most engine covers are the bane of mechanics everywhere, but they are no match for an impact driver *(Author)*

Screwdrivers are an integral part of any tool kit, with a varied assortment of long ones, short ones, fat ones, and thin ones being a must. Some screws tend to be inaccessible to all except the right screwdriver, but these latter are always seemingly a sale item in five and dime, or hardware stores, where a good selection can be picked up for very little money.

Phillips or cross-head screws used widely throughout engines are the bane of many novice mechanics not possessing one handy tool - an impact driver. Extremely hard to remove, with even the correct Phillips screwdriver, an impact makes light work of removing a dozen or so cross-heads, and more importantly does not destroy the cross slot in the screw, thus making reassembly easy. All impacts are constructed basically the same, with a coiled internal spring supplying the rotational force necessary to loosen the screw. The procedure is simple. Attach the correct bit, place into the screw and rap the end of the impact with a hammer to release the spring. Presto — the screw is loose. Impacts also tighten screws and bits are also available to cope with the most stubborn of ordinary slotted screws.

Nothing is harder or more frustrating than trying to remove a part for which the correct puller is not available. Flywheel magnetos and clutches are usually the main areas on which this frustration is vented and it more often than not results in damage costing more than the purchase price of a simple puller. So check out any special tools needed to strip an engine before attempting it. You'll save yourself a lot of money.

It isn't possible to list every tool you may, or will require, for as previously mentioned, your tool kit will grow with your needs. However, a hacksaw, pliers, vice grips, files, timing light, compression tester, feeler gages, duct tape, odd nuts and bolts, hose clamps and locking wire should all be included, as at some time or another they will be needed.

Odds and ends are also an important part of a tool kit, and it is surprising what items can be utilized before they are dumped in the trash can. Here are two examples; no doubt you will think of others.

1. Cut old inner tubes radially to make excellent rubber bands, which can be used in emergencies. Rear brake pedal not completely returning to the off position? Use an inner tube rubber band as a temporary spring.
2. Catch those old cosmetic tweezers before they are thrown out. Yes, everyone drops a part into a partially assembled engine at some time and tweezers may just save the day.

ANCILLARY EQUIPMENT

The end of the list is in sight. A couple of items still remain while others which only add to your comfort can be overlooked, begged, borrowed, or their purchase put back until some time in the future.

Gas stops are not required in flat track racing, thus the need for an approved refuelling container, such as the quick fill type used in road racing, is eliminated. A gas can holding enough fuel for a day's racing is a requirement, and one with a spring loaded discharge cap can be purchased at most automobile accessory stores.

Flat track bikes, like many racing bikes, have no sidestands and require some simple steel stand to remain in a vertical position. Chances are if you buy a used machine a stand may be thrown in to sweeten the deal, but whereas a stand seems such a mundane thing, try to work on a bike without one! The milk crate, a favorite substitute for so many years, works well, yet

Come slide with us

Above A good stand is necessary for keeping the machine upright at either the race track or in the workshop; the best types utilize a long lever to avoid lifting the machine *(Author)*

Below A Honda generator at work between races, charging the battery of a machine with no generating system *(Author)*

even this lowly object has undergone changes in the interests of progress, and the plastic crate of today is not nearly as structurally sound or enduring as the old metal type. With no access to welding or metal working equipment, a last resort might be a frame manufacturer, as most produce stands for their respective frames.

Owning a machine with no charging system can pose problems, as it is necessary to keep on hand at least one additional charged up battery in case the one in use cannot last the day. Conventional small motorcycle batteries do not hold great charges of electricity so it is prudent to know for how long a particular battery can be used, before being switched. All sorts of problems can and do develop with batteries, not the least of which is coasting to an ignominious halt with one that is supposedly fully charged. Many riders circumvent these problems by using a Honda generator. Very compact and completely self-contained, with its own extremely quiet gasoline engine, the unit is put to work in between races, charging the onboard battery. While your own generator may seem like an expensive toy, remember they also produce house current sufficient to run power tools to make repairs, or run appliances when travelling.

Come slide with us

An easier alternative to the hand or foot pump is a tank filled with a plentiful supply of air *(Author)*

Many advances have been made in tire technology over the last few years, consequently the air pump is now often thought of as a redundant piece of equipment. But to the racer on a budget, a pump can be the difference between riding and not. The scene never changes. The rear tire always goes flat when you have no spare wheel. If there is a spare, it has the wrong tire on it. At some stage a tire pump is needed to inflate the either swapped or mended tube. A search through the pits finally turns up a pump which lets more air escape to atmosphere than actually enters the tube. On that kind of day you are justified in thinking that it might have been better to have stayed in bed — and all for the sake of a pump! If you still aren't convinced, needing an additional reason to buy, consider your own vehicle. One day that pump may just get you out of a tight spot, should the spare be flat. To complement the pump don't forget a couple of tire irons, a repair kit or spare tube, and a pressure gauge.

An old piece of tarpaulin or canvas may seem an odd thing to take along yet it can be an invaluable aid towards remaining sane. The ground is not an ideal place for working on motorcycles and small parts and screws tend to become camouflaged when placed on the dirt. And it always seems to be that the part which is lost is the one you cannot get along without! The canvas or tarpaulin strategically placed under the bike will help alleviate the problem of trying to locate parts if you have to work on the engine in the pits.

Most families already own either an ice chest or insulated Thermos jug, which probably doesn't get as much use as it could, so borrowing it can save a few bucks. Racing can be warm work, especially on a hot day, so keep cold water or juices available. Any water left over can be used to wash away the dust at the end of the day.

Hopefully, you will not be working every minute of race day on the bike. There should be more than enough time to just sit relaxing in the sun watching a race, or the girls go by. A collapsible aluminum chair is the best choice here, for apart from the ground, there isn't anything else to sit on. Chances are there could be a couple of chairs in the garden or stored away in the basement, just waiting to be used. Go to it!

And now you're all set to prepare the bike.

Come slide with us

PREPARING THE MACHINE

The temptation to go out for a test ride immediately is inherent in anyone who has ever bought a competition mount. Indeed, riding was the object of the exercise in plonking down all that money, more especially so if the bike happens to be your first. If there is a place to try out the machine, and you are relatively sure it requires no work to bring it up to scratch, then by all means ride it — conservatively. There is no need to go into a long piece about whether or not your used machine is safe to ride, for ninety nine percent of them are, and you'll have discarded the other one percent anyway. No self-respecting rider or shop would sell a defective machine knowingly, yet if out practising without checking everything over first, it is worthwhile being prepared for anything untoward happening. Circulate slowly for a few laps, to make sure everything works correctly then, and only then, increase speed.

A few laps at a fast lick should satisfy the racer in you and may also serve to see what, if anything, has to be done to the bike before actually racing. Time has to be set aside each week for preparation, but being new to the sport and knowing little mechanically the novice tends to leave well alone. After all, if you don't know what to look for or do, how can it be done? We can cover the routine maintenance, which should be tackled every week, in a moment. In the meantime, back to the initial ride.

The first few laps were probably a definite happening, with all your concentration needed just to get around, yet you may have noticed how uncomfortable the handlebar position was, and man, those footpegs are weird! That first ride did more than satisfy the racer's urge. It served to show the controls must be tailored to your build.

National Number 20, John Gennai, closely followed by 84, Walt Foster *(Bob Jackson)*

There is no set position for handlebars as what suits one does not suit another. To find your most comfortable handlebar position, sit on the machine with arms outstretched and elbows slightly bent. If, when lowering the arms, your hands drop around the grips, the 'bars are great for you. Should you be stretching, twist 'em back. Conversely, if you are pushed too far to the rear of the seat, twist 'em forward. After racing the machine, you could possibly find the handlebars are too wide by an inch or so, but be sure, for once cut off, the metal cannot be replaced.

No problems exist with the throttle and the clutch lever is an easy devil. Position it radially where most comfortable, with the ball end slightly inboard of the end of the 'bar. This ensures the fingers can take full advantage of the leverage and, should you go down, lessens the chances of bending or breaking the lever.

The gear and brake lever on the right hand side of the motorcycle may seem an awkward combination but it isn't really. As the right side footpeg is positioned further back than on conventional machines, the gear lever will have to be reached for, but then it is only used to get the motorcycle into top gear and then left alone throughout the race. The left footpeg may require repositioning, should it be found not to be in the most comfortable position. However, only time and experience will determine this. In general, go with any fixed settings and see how everything works out under actual racing conditions, before attempting any serious modifications.

The 'kill' switch, usually a button attached to the left handlebar, should be positioned so that the thumb can operate it while the hand remains around the grip. On machines which have a compression release fitted, this too must be operable from the grip.

Adjustment of the controls has purposely been left out, to be covered under regular maintenance, as adjustments should be made on a weekly basis.

With the bike tailored, it is time to begin a check and maintenance program. Should you keep putting the maintenance off until the last moment, just remember reliability is a product of careful preparation and is only a drag if you make it so. Granted when young there are more exciting things to do at night than work on a bike, but the 'bike heal thyself' attitude just doesn't cut it.

While the cycle parts can be covered quite comprehensively, only the simplest of engine adjustments are included. If you intend to do your own engine work a workshop manual plus further information from manufacturers (and tuners regarding any trick parts installed), will be required. The majority of motorcycle manufacturers print manuals for their engines, and publishers, most notably Clymer and Chilton, (and last but not least, Haynes, the publishers of this book), print manuals for practically every engine currently produced.

As you become more proficient at racing, chances are you will start looking for the slight edge which could improve your performance. If your used bike was purchased locally it has more than likely been used at a local track and is probably 'dialed in' somewhere near correct, although you may ultimately decide some changes have to be made. It is impossible to tell you what springs you should be using or what kind of dampening response you like. All that maintenance can cover is what areas need constant attention. So race with the equipment you have until the natural progression of your own experience allows you to make intelligent evaluations. By that time you will have also befriended other racers, who will be more than ready to help by adding their suggestions to your own.

Flat track racing is not a wet weather sport yet machines do become grimy with dust sticking to almost every external part, and dirt adhering like cement to the front portions of the machine. Any maintenance is best done on a clean machine for two reasons: (1) The dust and grime doesn't get in the engine if covers have to be taken off, and (2) any defect such as a crack in a case is more easily spotted without the coating of dust. Hence the first job should be a thorough hosing and washing of the machine. The ingestion of water into the engine can be avoided by rubber banding a plastic bag over the carburetor, while not directly hosing a cover hiding the flywheel magneto will lessen the chances of water entering through there.

Breaking up the work into sections is the easiest way to tackle any maintenance, as haphazardly going from one place to another usually results in something being forgotten. In what order the jobs are done is immaterial, just so long as you touch all bases, but obviously any serious engine work requiring ordering of new parts should not be left to the end of the week.

ENGINE LUBRICATION
Four stroke
Lubricating oil is the life blood of any four-stroke engine but unlike our own, it does wear

Come slide with us

Ray Beck (12z) and Chuck Palmgren (38) *(Bob Jackson)*

out. Regular oil changes increase the life of any engine and although prevention may seem a trifle expensive, it is always cheaper than the cost of rebuilding a worn out engine. How often is regular? Some riders change oil after every meeting, others after every two, maybe three. If you are not making the semi or final then the oil isn't being worked to its limit, so to begin with, base your oil changes on your performance. The more races you ride in, the quicker the oil will wear out and need replacing.

Irrespective of whether the oil is carried in the frame or a tank, there is an oil filter somewhere in the system, which must not be forgotten. At every oil change it must be washed out and cleaned in gasoline, or replaced, if a throwaway type. If the machine is fitted with an oil cooler, check the hoses for cracks or looseness and ensure the core is not blocked with clumps of earth.

The oil in the gearbox and primary drive should also be changed with some regularity. Gearboxes take a lot of punishment, the proof being the metallic filings found in the oil. In many machines the primary drive oil also lubricates the clutch. The resulting wear shows up in the oil as sludge from the clutch plates and metal from the gears or chain.

Two-stroke

All two-stroke engines, whether lubricated mechanically or with a gas/oil mist, operate on a total loss basis. The oil never circulates as in a four-stroke, it simply lubricates and is then expelled through the exhaust. The main consideration with two-strokes is to make sure fresh, clean oil, is used in either the gas mix or oil tank.

The gearbox and primary drive will, however, require the same attention outlined for the four-stroke engine.

Conspicuous by its absence is any reference as to what type or brand of oil should be used in your racing machine. This is because it seems everyone agrees to differ on what is best. In general, mineral oils are the heavy favorites.

Oils can be broken down into three types: castor (or bean) based, mineral, and synthetic. Castor oils were used for many years, probably the best known being Castrol R, but two developments over recent years have lessened its use. The first of these was undoubtedly the improvements made in mineral oils. Because of the high temperatures generated in racing engines, it is necessary to use an oil which lubricates as well at the end of a race as it does at the start. While castor oil filled this bill perfectly, minerals never did, for when hot they thinned out like water, with a corresponding drop in lubricating properties. Progress by the oil

Come slide with us

companies has now changed all that to where riders find mineral oils more than adequate for the job at hand. The second development which added to the demise of bean oil has been the rising price of beans, which in turn increased the cost of the oil dramatically to where everyone looked to alternatives.

Synthetic oils, though excellent, still have a long way to go before being generally accepted, and only with increased production can the price be reduced to a more palatable level.

Most oil companies produce a top of the line mineral oil and some even a mineral racing oil, but as to what brand to use, that is up to you. Large oil companies have a reputation to uphold and their oils perform extremely well in all types of racing machinery. Many actively support racing of one type or another, consequently you can't go far wrong using their products. Another way is to check around the pits to see what everyone else uses, and don't be afraid to try different brands throughout your racing career for only by experimentation can you find what really works best.

CARBURETOR AND SPARK PLUG

Assuming that the engine is correctly jetted, both the carburetor and spark plug can be treated as separate entities for maintenance purposes.

As a general rule the carburetor will require only minor adjustments after being jetted initially. Problems do occur from time to time but a couple of preventative measures taken regularly can limit the areas of trouble, should the whole thing suddenly go out of 'sync'.

The correct float level measurement is important in any carburetor as too high can cause flooding; too low, fuel starvation. Most float bowls are easily removed without disturbing the carburetor body and the float level set to the manufacturer or tuner's specifications. By removing the bowl carefully, any sediment accumulation can be readily seen in the bottom. Rinse this out with gas plus any filters in either the gas line or at the entry point of the carburetor. Also check the needle shut off valve for any signs of wear. This will show up as an indented ring on the cone shaped surface of the valve. Finish by ensuring the carburetor body is tightly bolted onto the engine, thus eliminating problems which might occur from an air leak and a resulting lean mixture.

The plug should be removed each week, cleaned and regapped, or replaced, if worn. When tightening into an aluminum head, apply only 14ft.lb. of torque.

'Reading' spark plugs and correctly jetting carburetors is an art which has to be worked at to be mastered. A lot of written information exists on the subject, some of it good and some

Former Grand National Champion Mert Lawwill, still one of the quickest and probably the smoothest flat tracker of them all, always makes it look too easy (Bob Jackson)

Come slide with us

bad. If you need help go to the right source, write to the Champion Spark Plug Company, PO Box 910, Toledo, Ohio 43601 and request their literature on jetting and spark plugs.

IGNITION TIMING

Checking the ignition timing, though often a nightmare to those attempting it for the first time, should be done on a weekly basis. It really isn't so complicated once you understand what is happening inside the engine. Very simply, an electrical charge, either generated inside the engine by a rotating magneto, or supplied from an external source such as a battery, is boosted in voltage through a coil and applied to the spark plug at just the right time to ignite the atomized gasoline for maximum power. Part of the ignition system is a switch that determines the exact time to apply the charge to the spark plug. It is this part, the points, which requires constant monitoring, for as with any mechanical device, the points wear and require adjustment. Should your machine be fitted with a pointless ignition system, you will be spared this task, as the ignition is set at the factory, requiring no further adjustment throughout its life. However, many manufacturers still use conventional ignition systems and these comments are directed to the owners of such systems.

Replacing the points is easily done by removing and remembering what goes where. After doing it a few times, it becomes an easy job. Correctly gapping the points comes with experience in using feeler gages and achieving the right amount of 'feel' for the gap required. It is worth spending time learning this skill as one thousandth of an inch discrepancy at the points is equivalent to one degree of crankshaft rotation. In English, this means that if the points don't have the correct gap, the engine is not firing at the exact time it should, for maximum power.

Timing the ignition is best done with a timing light for it reduces the job to a few minutes work and is extremely accurate. Almost all ignition systems can be set with a timing light, owner and aftermarket manuals explaining in detail, with photographs, how this is achieved.

AIR CLEANERS

Gasoline will not burn without the presence of air, vast quantities of which must pass through the air cleaner and carburetor to reach the combustion chamber. A blocked air cleaner will greatly impair performance but this can be avoided with periodic cleanings. Foam and fabric filters should be cleaned in solvent and then re-oiled, prior to use, to ensure effective filtering. Paper filters must be renewed, when blocked.

LOCK OR SAFETY WIRING

Oil dropped on a race track can pose problems for anyone who slides through it at sixty or seventy miles an hour. Luckily this seldom happens. Even more seldom is the cause, a loose

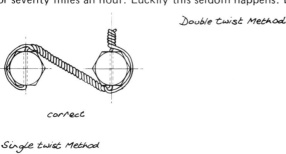

Double twist Method

correct

Single twist Method

Fr.

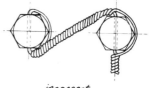

incorrect

Always twist the wire so that it tends to tighten rather than loosen the bolt. Never twist the wire too tight or it will break now or later. Use ·032" diameter stainless steel wire on bolts above ¼" diameter; ·020" diameter on ¼" diameter and less.

Figure 3. The correct and incorrect ways of safety wiring *(Author)*

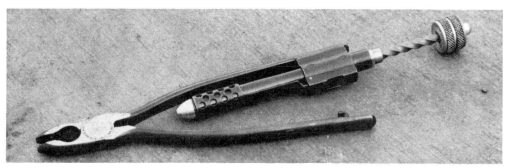

Robinson safety wire twisters make light and neat work of safety wiring *(Author)*

drain plug, which unscrews with vibration. The reason is, of course, that all drain plugs have to be lock wired to prevent such problems. After any oil change in either the engine, gearbox, primary case or front forks, the drain plugs will need rewiring and though twisting the wire can be done by hand, it is more neatly and quickly achieved with a wire twisting tool, available from stores or tool suppliers which cater to the racing fraternity.

In the event the oil is not changed, it is good practise to check under the bike anyhow, to ensure the wired plugs are as they should be.

WHEELS AND BRAKES

Wheels are frequently overlooked when preparing a machine, yet a bad or dry bearing can absorb a lot of horsepower. Spin each wheel when clear of the ground, to make sure it rotates freely. Check for sideplay, and replace or lubricate as needed.

Stresses and strains cause spokes to loosen, especially when wheels are new, but care should be taken in 'nipping' them up, for it is easy to keep tightening and suddenly find the wheel out of true. Unless you are proficient at truing wheels, exercise caution when tightening up loose spokes.

Check the disk brake caliper action by spinning the wheel and pressing down on the brake lever, making sure the mechanism releases when the lever is released. A precautionary glance at brake pad thickness, and reservoir fluid level, are worthwhile habits to get into for your own safety and peace of mind.

CHAIN ADJUSTMENT AND CARE

For many reasons, a chain is not the ideal method of driving the rear wheel of a high powered motorcycle, but stuck with it we are, until something better comes along. Chain is expensive, but with careful adjustment and lubrication, replacement can be kept to a minimum. The life of the sprockets also depends on how well the chain is adjusted and aligned, and different kinds of wear on the teeth are usually indications of maladjustment. The correct amount of slack in the bottom run is critical, for a chain too tight will wear deeply into the sprockets and could cause premature failure of the gearbox. Too slack, the chain will jump the teeth, rendering both sprockets and chain useless in a very short time. And, if the front and rear sprockets are not in line, the sides of the sprockets will wear rapidly, as will the chain.

To promote quick sprocket (and tire) changes in the limited amount of practise time available, the normal master or split link is used to join the rear chain. This makes maintenance an easy task and the chain should be removed, cleaned, and lubricated regularly with one of the many lubricants which penetrate the rollers. Keep a weather eye on the adjustment at the races, lubricate once or twice during the day, and your chain will give good service.

SHOCK ABSORBERS

Shocks do not usually require weekly maintenance, just a quick check of the dampening is necessary once in a while. With the spring removed, there should be resistance to movement of the spindle in either direction. Many shocks are rebuildable so if yours require work, chances are a rebuild kit is available.

Come slide with us

FRONT FORKS

Forks, like shocks, require very little week to week maintenance. The oil will need changing occasionally and the oil seals have to be replaced when more than usual amounts of oil are seen on the chrome legs. The Neoprene boot atop the seals is very effective in cleaning the leg before the seals pass over it and this contributes to seal life. The boots should be replaced if at all suspected of doing a lousy wiping job.

IMPORTANT ODDS AND ENDS

The majority of the work now done, it is time to run a final check over the machine. Cables usually require some adjustment, as they are constantly stretching, so let's start there.

The throttle cable should be adjusted to where approximately 1/16 in of slack (or lash) exists at the drum before the slide in the carburetor begins to move upwards off its seat. Anything less than this will usually result in the engine delivering power, even when the throttle is completely closed.

The clutch cable should also be adjusted, with slack at the lever (1/8 in), for this ensures no pressure is causing a slipping condition, the quickest way known to man to burn up clutch plates.

Before the tools are finally put away, be sure to spend five minutes tightening nuts and bolts. Vibration, the bane of every motorcyclist, has a way of loosening the best locking nuts, and left unchecked, can be both dangerous and costly. Check the engine mounting bolts especially, as loose bolts here can result in damaged castings, which are expensive to replace and will necessitate a complete strip down. Wheels and handlebars are two other areas on which your life depends, so pay attention to these and any bolt on items, such as coils, which tend to be forgotten once installed.

One item which has been left until now need only be taken care of at the start of your racing career and a few times after that. What is it? Number plates. If your flat tracker was bought used, chances are the plates were left on it. Make sure they are the right color and buy some stick on numbers.

Needing only gas and oil the bike is ready! Before all the tools are put away, make sure it runs, trying not to annoy the neighbors too much.

Let's go racing.

Following is a list of manufacturers and suppliers of riding apparel used by flat track racers. The list is by no means complete but these are some of the producers mentioned in the text of the previous chapter. Some items are distributed by other companies in various areas of the country.

Leathers

ABC Leathers
9802 S. Atlantic Avenue
South Gate, Calif. 90280
Tel: (213) - 564 - 1715

Bates Industries
701 W. Cowles Street
Long Beach, Calif. 90801
Tel: (213) - 435 - 6551

Helmets

Bell
Bell Helmets Inc.
15301 Shoemaker Avenue
Norwalk, Calif. 90650
Tel: (213) - 921 - 9451

KRW
Trabaca Products
3170 Airway Avenue
Costa Mesa, Calif. 92626
Tel: (714) - 556 - 6965

Rebcor
Rebcor Inc.
3300 Dixie Highway
Fairfield, Ohio. 45014
Tel: (513) - 867 - 8000

Steel Skid Shoe

Maely Enterprises
Route 2, Box 75B
8530 Bedford Motorway
Corona, Calif. 91720
Tel: (714) - 735 - 0540

Protective Equipment

Jim Davis Motosport
PO Box 1002
Burbank, Calif. 91505
Tel: (213) - 762 - 2045

Come slide with us

The riders' meeting *(Bob Jackson)*

10 Today's the day

'IF YOU TURN LEFT AT THE NEXT INTERSECTION YOU CAN SEE THE TRACK: YES, THERE IT IS. JUST FOLLOW ALL THOSE OTHER VANS. MAN, IT'S WARM TODAY.'

The line of vehicles heading for the infield creeps forward until each passes through the gate in the chain link fence, then on across the dirt surface of the track (at which everyone casts a cursory glance) into the rapidly filling pit area. Only then does the convoy split off into different directions, some to join friends already there, others to find and set up in an uncrowded spot.

'How about parking somewhere in the middle then you can see and hear everything that's going on.' ...... 'Yeah, this is fine.'

With the van finally stopped neither moves. They sit there soaking up the activity to the left, right, and to the front of them. Bikes being carefully unloaded, bikes being gassed and oiled, bikes having some last minute chore attended to. Riders pulling on leathers, tying boots, cleaning faceshields, or just sitting, leaning, talking to passers by and friends. And then there are the good looking girls in tight jeans and cut off jeans, and halter tops and T-shirts.

'Wow! Did you see that?' No reply. 'Hey, you must be nervous if you didn't see that. Come on, there's no need to be uptight, I'll help you as much as I can. It'll soon become old hat. Let's boogie on over and get you signed in first.' An afterthought, 'Jeez! I can't believe you didn't see that.'

Over at the sign-in table riders are filling in entry forms then joining the short line to await processing. The walk back to the van is somewhat more relaxed, time enough to tense up again later.

'We'd better unload so you can change. They want the trucks out of here.'

While some semblance of order is still being brought to the pile of equipment removed from the van, an obviously self conscious figure resplendent in new riding gear tries vainly (to his mind) to merge unobtrusively into the scene, after exiting through the back doors of the van.

In the pit to the right a head is peering down through a frame into the mouth of a crankcase, while another is aimed at the sky through the cylinder. To the left an obviously ready competitor sits reading a weekly motorcycle tabloid.

'I told you no one would take any notice of you. Do you see anyone staring at you?' ...... 'Okay. Drive your van out and I'll meet you with the bike over there where the crowd has formed, that's where the scrutineer hangs out.'

The man does his job quickly and efficiently. Drain plugs are checked for safety wiring then the rest of the machine checked over for loose parts and sticking controls. A small decal placed in the corner of the front number plate, a nod of the head and another hurdle is over.

Back in the pits the machine is lifted onto its stand to await practice.

'When practice starts you'll be let out a few at a time and flagged in after a few laps. Keep going back to the staging area to get as much practice as you can, without tiring yourself out.

Today's the day

Don't go too fast first time out, build up your speed a little at a time.' ...... 'If they want to pass they can go around the outside ......' The last part of the sentence is lost as engines burst into life. The bike is pushed off the stand, an obvious indication to get ready.

Some time later when practice is officially over the motorcycle is again lifted onto the stand, and a grinning face appears from beneath a dirt splattered full coverage helmet. A cup of ice cold water offered is quickly emptied in one gulp but the grin remains.

'Not bad you're beginning to get the hang of it.' The grin persists. 'Bike working out okay' ...... 'Everything seems alright from here. I stood on that corner watching you for a while. Towards the end you were getting around quite respectably.' He held up a hand with the thumb and forefinger formed into a circle. 'Well let's clean you up and check over the bike. Your leathers don't look quite so new now do they?' They both laugh.

The bike is readied in between friends dropping by. He is introduced to them, beginning for the first time to feel part of what was taking place, rather than as an outsider looking in.

Everything is tight and the chain is okay. You put in the gas, I checked the cables. There's one little job you didn't do' ...... 'Clean your faceshield. Better do it now before you forget' ...... 'No, the heats are only four laps, you won't need any tearoffs. They'll be calling a rider's meeting soon so I'm going for something to eat. Coming?' ...... 'Okay, I understand, I'll see you in a few minutes.'

Although he busies himself checking the machine, the minutes drag by like hours. The incessant talking of his friend would have annoyed him at any other time and he would have told him so. Today, well today was different. In the only way he knew how, Charlie was

Above The ideal pit; a place for everything, and everything in its place *(Author)*

Below Routine maintenance *(Author)*

148

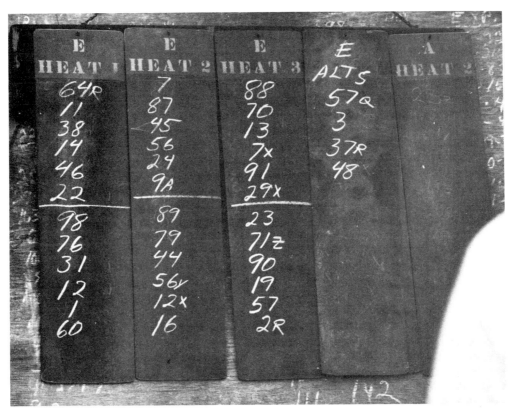

You'll find your heat race on the board near the start *(Bob Jackson)*

trying to make it as easy as possible for him.

'Sure you don't want a bite?' The hot dog is thrust in his face as he kneels beside the machine. He shakes his head.

A voice over the public address system announces a riders' meeting in five minutes. A few begin to trickle over to the starting area followed by the majority as soon as the officials can be seen to be there. In just a few minutes the whole thing is over, with everyone assured the rules will be enforced, the track is in good shape, the first heat is due on the line in ten minutes and that each rider can find his respective heat, if he hasn't already done so, on the board to their backs.

Today's the day

'Well, well, lookee here, you're in the first heat. You had better get ready' ...... 'Ah, come on now, this is what you came for. You're all nervous because this is your first time. I know this doesn't help but everyone here went through the same thing, and most are still nervous at the start. During the race you'll be concentrating so hard there won't be time to be nervous. Now you've got the starting procedure down pat?' ...... 'That's alright, we'll go over it again. Line up on the starting line where they tell you, facing the wrong direction. When the man tells you all to start, push your bike; I'll be with you so don't worry. Ride to the last corner and back to warm it up. Line up a yard or so back from the starting line, pop the bike in neutral until the starter sees everyone is ready. When he stands on the platform with the flag above his head, put the bike in gear and move forward to the line. Put your weight well forward over the handlebars otherwise you'll do a huge wheelie. When everyone is ready he will drop the flag to his side, but don't go then or you will be placed back on the penalty line. Go when he waves the flag. It seems like ages to wait I know, but it's only seconds.'

With butterflies leaping around in his stomach, and his helmet luckily hiding the nervousness he feels, they both push the bike over to the pit entrance, then join the other riders out on the track. Lined up in their respective positions facing the wrong way, with mechanics standing to the rear to help push, they await the signal to start the machines.

Suddenly, the first motorcycle moves, and then the second, barking into life within a few yards followed by some of the others. Just as he forces his weight to the handlebars, a hand on the shoulder stops him. Turning, a friendly face comes up close to his own. He feels the slap on the back barely making out the words over the noise.

'Hey! Good luck.'

A hamburger with everything, french fries and a coke to go *(Bob Jackson)*

Today's the day

Good Luck *(Bob Jackson)*

Appendix 1 ———————————

A LIST OF COMPANIES WHO PARTICIPATED IN THE 1976 AMA CAMEL PRO SERIES CONTINGENCY AWARDS PROGRAM

ABC/Bell Custom Leathers
Bates Industries, Inc.
Beck/Arnley Corporation
Bell Helmets, Inc.
Bel-Ray Company, Inc.
Champion Spark Plug Company
Diamond Chain Company
Dunlop Tire & Rubber Company
Interpart Corporation
Goodyear Tire & Rubber Company
KRW Helmets/Trabaca Products, Inc.
Lectron Products, Inc.
Michelin Tire Corporation
Pirelli Tire Corporation
Rebcor Helmets Inc.
Marubeni American Corp./Red Wing Group
Sure-Fire Distributing Company
Torco Oil Company
Vista-sheen, Inc.

Appendix 2 ———————————

THE FOLLOWING IS THE 1977 CAMEL PRO GRAND NATIONAL SERIES SCHEDULE

Date	Location	Type
1/29	Houston Astrodome Houston, Texas.	TT
1/29	Houston Astrodome Houston, Texas.	ST
3/13	Daytona International Speedway Daytona Beach, Florida.	RR
3/20	Charlotte Motor Speedway Harrisburg, NC.	RR
5/15	Santa Clara County Fairgrounds San Jose, Calif.	M
5/22	Oklahoma State Fairgrounds Oklahoma City, Okla.	½ M

Date	Location	Type			
6/4	Louisville Downs Fairgrounds Louisville, Kentucky.	½ M			
6/11	Delaware State Fairgrounds Harrington, De.	½ M			
6/19	Bryar Motorsports Park Loudon, NH.	RR			
6/24	Santa Fe Park Hinsdale, Illinois.	TT			
6/26	Ohio State Fairgrounds Columbus, Ohio	½ M			
7/3	Texas World Speedway College Station, Texas.	RR			
7/9	Santa Clara County Fairgrounds San Jose, Calif.	½ M			
7/10	Sears Point International Raceway Sonoma, Calif.	RR			
7/16	Castle Rock Fairgrounds Castle Rock, Washington	TT			
7/23	Ascot Park Gardena, Calif.	TT			
7/31	DuQuoin Fairgrounds DuQuoin, Illinois.	M			
8/5	Sante Fe Park Hinsdale, Illinois.	ST			
8/7	Peoria Motorcycle Clubgrounds Peoria, Illinois.	TT			
8/14	Vigo County Fairgrounds Terre Haute, Indiana	½ M			
8/21	Pocono International Raceway Mt. Pocono, Pennsylvania.	RR			
8/27	Indiana State Fairgrounds Indianapolis, Indiana	M			
8/28	Indiana State Fairgrounds Indianapolis, Indiana	M			
9/4	Orange County Fair Speedway Middletown, NY.	½ M			
9/11	New York State Fairgrounds Syracuse, NY.	M			
9/17	Raceway Park Toledo, Ohio.	½ M			
9/25	Santa Clara County Fairgrounds San Jose, Calif.	M	KEY		
10/2	Riverside Raceway Riverside, Calif.	RR	TT ST	Tourist Trophy Short Track
10/8 or 10/9	Ascot Park Gardena, Calif.	½ M	RR ½ M	Road Race Half Mile
10/9 *	Cal Expo Sacramento, Calif.	M	M	Mile

*Pending contract with Cal Expo. If contract is not received, Ascot will run on October 9.